Palaces of Seoul

Yi Dynasty Palaces in Korea's Capital City

Text and Photographs

by

Edward B. Adams

SEOUL INTERNATIONAL PUBLISHING HOUSE

Yongdong P.O. Box 629, Seoul, Korea 135 Tel: 542-9308, 543-6010

First printing in June 1972
Fourth printing in October 1, 1987
Copyright © 1972 by Seoul International Publishing House
All rights reserved. No part of this book may be reproduced in any form except
for brief quotation in a review without permission from the publisher.
Library Congress Catalog Card Number 72-77238
Printed and bound by Samhwa Printing Co., Ltd., Seoul, Korea
Publisher's Registration No. 16-4
Yongdong P.O. Box 629, Seoul, Korea 135
Tel: 542-9308, 543-6010
Price: ₩ 7,000

To
Princess Yi Pang-ja
and
Mr. Kyu Lee
Grandson of King Ko-jong

CONTENTS

CHAPTER I

CHAPTER II

CHAPTER VI

Chongmyo (Royal Ancestral Shrine) 145

APPENDIX 174

Photographs Acknowledgment

The author is extremely grateful to Princess Yi Pang-ja and other members of the royal household for the use of many historical pictures. The pictures taken by other than the author are duly recognized in the captions.

FOREWORD

The *Palaces of Seoul* by Edward B. Adams is a pleasing blend of guidebook and history of the city's palaces. Quiet gardens, regal architecture and legend-laden environs represent five centuries of the Yi Dynasty era where the kings and queens played out their parts in the pageant of Korean history.

I became aware of Mr. Adams' research many years ago while he was preparing the manuscript for *Through Gates of Seoul* which was published in the summer of 1971. I eagerly followed his work and assisted in many areas where revisions and clarifications were necessary. Our personal friendship has now deepened as he continues his pursuit in the cultural and historical heritage of our country.

The Seoul area between the Han River and Samgak-san was settled prior to recorded history. Recently the site of a paleolithic village was discovered along the banks of the Han River. Also during the Three Kingdoms period this Han River valley was fought over and used as an annex capital during different eras. In the late fourteenth century Yi T'ae-jo officially made Hanyang (Seoul) his capital and constructed Kyongbok Palace. Several additional palaces were built some of which were destroyed during the Hideyoshi invasion of 1592.

For many years Mr. Adams has been avidly taking photographs of the ceremonial pomp and court dress of palace rites. Many of these photos, some of which are impossible to obtain today, appear in *Palaces of Seoul.* His friendship with the surviving members of the royal family has won him entrance to many ceremonies seldom seen by Koreans or foreigners.

We can not dismiss our impression of the author's pride in the heritage of the Korean people and his optimism in the future of the land of his birth. For three generations his family has played a part in Korean history. His grandfather, James Edward Adams, was a pioneer missionary, reaching Korean soil on May 29, 1895, not long before the assassination of Queen Min. A stone tablet erected by the Korean people in Taegu bears record to the founding of his mission work in that city. The author's father and the author were both born in Taegu City.

Mr. Adams has written *Palaces of Seoul* to help foreigners and Koreans to better understand and learn of our country's history and folklore. The historical remains in the Seoul Palaces are associated with prominent personalities. The author's interjections of historical facts or legends about these places add great interest, for in them we find romance, tragedy and even nostalgia.

Not only should this book be read by foreigners but by the Koreans themselves. A detailed book in English on the *Palaces of Seoul* and the ceremony associated with these Yi Dynasty palaces has filled a long-felt need. It is not only an illustrated guidebook of Seoul's historic palace surroundings, but also brings these surroundings to life with a delightfully revealing personal introduction to palace history.

Dr. Hwang Su-young
President, Dongguk University
Former Director of the National Museum

INTRODUCTION

Palaces of Seoul is an inexpensive book designed to aid the inquisitive tourist or resident of Korea who is interested in a comprehensive historical account of the existing palaces of Seoul. For the first-time visitor, the architecture is breathtaking. I honestly can not remember how many times I have wandered through the palaces during the various seasons of the year. Whether it be in the silence of winter with snow-laden tile roofs or during a crowded autumn Sunday afternoon, I have always found numerous hours of rewarding enjoyment. It is hard to say which season is best. Seoulites throng to the palaces on the weekends in spring and fall but during the week few people are seen along the hidden paths and among the painfully silent walls of old structures which emanate the grandeur and architectural expressiveness of centuries ago.

Most of the manuscript material for *Palaces of Seoul* can be found in Vol. I of *Through Gates of Seoul* published in the fall of 1970. In the first edition photographs were included by sections portraying palace architecture with the many designated treasures located within the palace walls. Also sections were given to depict the ceremonial tradition, funeral rites of Korea's last royalty, early palace scenes and royal portraits taken during the first part of this century.

In the 1982 revised edition most of the rare photographs have been kept but many additional color plates have been used to make the revised edition of *Palaces of Seoul* a more attractive publication. In addition to a different format, art paper was used rather than woodfree paper of the earlier edition.

To render Korean names and words into the Roman alphabet, a modified form of the McCune-Reischauer system of romanization is used without the diacritical marks. Some deviation was made from this system because of personal preference and the belief that the change would further aid the foreign reader in more accurately pronouncing Korean words.

One should be aware that there is also a different system of romanizations that was originally developed in 1960 by the Ministry of Education (MOE). Though the MOE system was finally abolished several years ago, many of the palace signs have not yet been changed. This will cause some concern to foreigners trying to pronounce Korean names correctly. Fortunately for tourists, the government has now officially accepted the McCune-Reischauer system of romanization. To illustrate this confusion; Toksu Palace was written Deogsoo and Pugak Mountain became Bugag.

To avoid the many problems inherent in the different romanization systems the newcomer should try to learn the Korean phonetic *han'gul* alphabet which is one of the easiest in the world. The Yi family of the Yi Dynasty is a common name in Korea. The Western variations of the spelling of Yi (李) are Lee, Rii, Rhee, Rhi, E, Li and Ea (and probably many more). This name is written in *han'gul* simply as (이).

The appendix should be helpful for those wishing to understand and know about the family ancestry of Yi Dynasty royalty. Also a listing of national and cultural treasures found at the palaces is included in the appendix.

I am hopeful that this small book will fill a need for the foreign tourists who will have little time in Seoul and can only spend a day to tour the palaces. For a brief moment they may catch glimpses of Korea's rich heritage as the worn path leads by intricately patterned wall designs or under the clay roof figurines which sit in eternal vigilance, warding off evil.

For those with more hours to spend the *Palaces of Seoul* will become a valuable resource of palace lore. I am certain that the hidden byways of the Secret Garden or architectural beauty of little known buildings will be more carefully studied with interest. As you rediscover the palaces of Seoul you will meet the Korean people. They are quick to laugh, frank and willing to become your friends.What better place than within the palaces to make an acquaintance! While living in Korea the spirit of the people will begin to show, a people proud of their heritage, progressive and willing to keep it but also share it with you if the interest is shown.

E. B. Adams

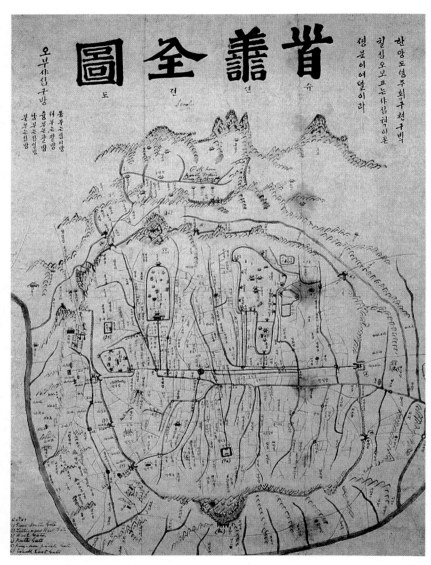

This particular map once belonged to Dr. J.W. Heron, who arrived to Korea in 1885 as a pioneer missionary doctor. The bell-shaped enclosure is Kyongbok Palace with the larger enclosure at right center the Ch'angdok Palace, Chongmyo and Ch'anggyong-won. Further east is the small shrine for Sa-do Seja (now SNU Hospital). The western enclosure is Kyonghui Palace (Mulberry Palace) which no longer exists and Sajik Shrine directly north. Toksu Palace, a more recently designated palace is not shown on this map. (The map is now owned by Dr. Samuel H. Moffett)

Kyongbok Palace

The Kyonghoe Pavilion
    soars higher,
After five centuries of
    dynasty glory.
The boom of the giant
    Chongno bell,
Oh, how clean and clear
    is each stroke.
The crystal sound crosses
    the courtyard,
And quickens the dusk in
    a quiet arbor.
I realize now that autumn
    has come,
As the paulownia has shed
    its leaves.
Cool and moist is the long
    night as,
Silk rain falls on the
    lotus pond.
With thoughts a thousand
    miles away,
Let the dusk and dawn
    pass me by.

Top: *A golden phoenix, symbol of the capital city of Seoul, city of Yi T'ae-jo, is a mythical bird which was probably suggested in China by the Argus pheasant, though in the matter of coloring, art has really far transcended nature. With a long tail and colorful plumage, the five hues of the phoenix represent the virtues of uprightness, decorum, wisdom, humanity and sincerity. Having become the royal badge of the queen, the phoenix when portrayed with the dragon (king) signifies a perfect marriage. This golden phoenix came from a lacquered jewelry box buried with concubine Kim Ssi on Sept. 28, 1735.*

Bottom: *This richly embroidered silk with phoenix and plum design was used as a state dress by Min, queen of King Ko-jong, probably in 1888. The extra yardage of this material with a number of other mementos, including hair jewelry, were presented as gifts by Queen Min to Mrs. John Heron M.D., wife of the royal physician who succeeded Horace Allen as superintendent of the Royal Hospital (now Severance Hospital).*

Right: *Twelve royal portraits were kept in Sonwon-jon of Ch'angdok Palace until 1950 at which time they were taken to Pusan for safe keeping during the Korean War. Unfortunately they were accidently burned in Pusan with only the portrait of Yong-jo (21st king) surviving the damaging fire. This portrait of Yong-jo is now kept at Ch'angdok Palace, and is one of the few extant portraits of Yi Dynasty kings.*

This portrait of King Ko-jong by an unknown artist is controversial because some authorities believe it is a copy of an earlier painting. It is now kept in the Ch'angdok Palace. The portrait was returned by Japan to Korea in 1967.

This portrait of King Ko-jong was donated to the National Museum by Lee Sang-ryong in December 1981. It was part of the collection of the late Lee Hong-kun the donator's father.

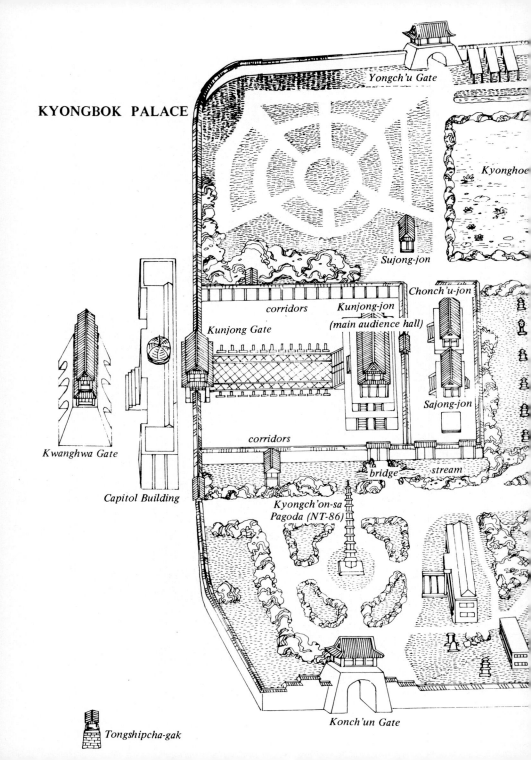

KYONGBOK PALACE

Yongch'u Gate

Kyonghoe

Sujong-jon

Chonch'u-jon

corridors

Kunjong Gate

Kunjong-jon
(main audience hall)

Kwanghwa Gate

Sajong-jon

corridors

bridge   stream

Capitol Building

Kyongch'on-sa
Pagoda (NT-86)

Tongshipcha-gak

Konch'un Gate

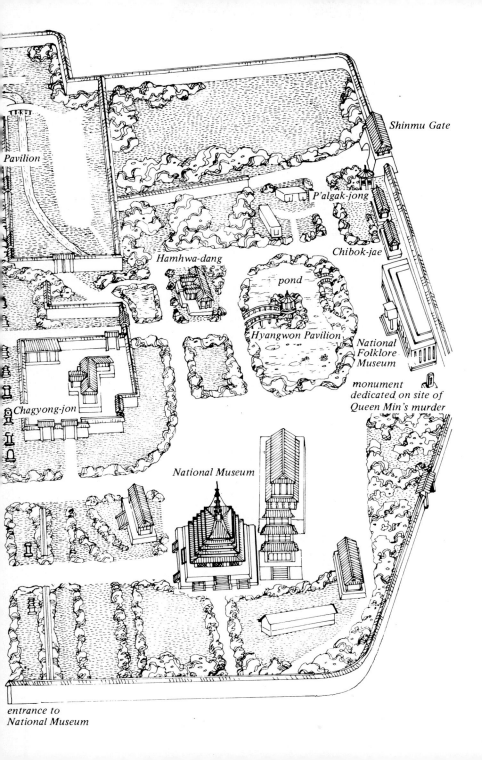

Pavilion

Shinmu Gate

P'algak-jong

Chibok-jae

Hamhwa-dang

pond

Hyangwon Pavilion

National
Folklore
Museum

monument
dedicated on site of
Queen Min's murder

Chagyong-jon

National Museum

entrance to
National Museum

LOCATION OF NATIONAL & CULTURAL TREASURES IN KYONGBOK PALACE

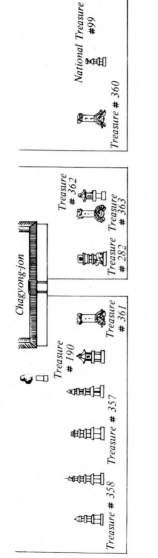

Stone Coffin of Prince Song-nyong and Placenta Container

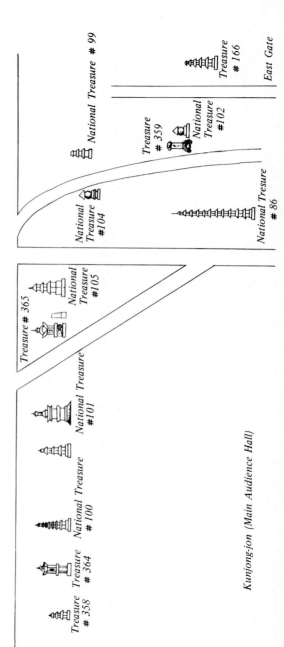

The only existing portrait of Yi T'ae-jo, first king of the Yi Dynasty, is enshrined in Kyonggi-jon at Chonju City. This shrine was constructed during the reign of King T'ae-jong, fifth son of Yi T'ae-jo. Hanyang, the capital city of Yi, was founded by Yi T'ae-jo over 500 years ago.

I. Kyongbok Palace-Beginning of the Yi Dynasty-1392

Hanyang, the capital city of the Yi Dynasty, was founded by Yi T'ae-jo over five hundred years ago. Within this town of Hanyang, now Seoul, Kyongbok Palace was built to be the residence and hub of dynastic power of the Chonju Yi family. The palace survived until the devastating Japanese invasion of 1592, when the entire palace was burned.

There are numerous legends and court records surrounding the founding of the Yi Dynasty in this small town cradled between Samgak-san and Nam-san. Before the birth of the dynasty, Shin-don, a Buddhist counterpart of Russia's Rasputin, had dominated the Koryo King Kong-min. Shin-don's power over the king existed because of the following episode:

King Kong-min had a frightening dream in which a monk saved him from an assassin's knife. Several days after the dream, the king met a priest closely resembling the monk who had rescued him in the nightmare. This priest was Shin-don, a monk of the lower classes who had been ostracized by his superiors. The king took him to the palace and bestowed lavish wealth and honors upon him. The excesses of this renegade priest were incredible and he was later banished to Suwon and eventually beheaded.

Meanwhile, because King Kong-min's beloved queen had died in child-birth and he had no heir, he took a son of one of Shin-don's concubines and told court officials the child was his. The king admitted that he had been visiting this girl and a child had been conceived. This story may have been invented to justify the Yi Dynasty takeover of the Koryo Dynasty.

In 1375 a trusted eunuch revealed to the king that one of his concubines was with child. The delighted ruler learned that the father was Hong, a court official. The king ordered Hong to be killed so that no one would know the child's paternity. Realizing this meant his death too, the eunuch hastened to tell Hong and together they plotted to assassinate the king. They stabbed him while he was in a drunken sleep. His ten-year-old son Shin-u (who was very likely the son of Shin-don) became king.

Shortly after King Shin-u ascended the throne, two court concubines each claimed to be the boy's mother, the more powerful being Han. She succeeded in having Pan-ya, the other claimant, arrested and sentenced to death by drowning. This was the severest penalty, since it was believed that the spirit of a drowned person seldom found peace. The story has been told that as Pan-ya stood on the river's edge she cried out her innocence and prophetically screamed that after her death a palace gate would fall as a sign that she was actually Shin-u's mother. As the young concubine sank beneath the waters, a gate in the capital fell and all knew, although too late, that she had told the truth.

The king's two most powerful generals, Ch'oe Yong and Yi Song-gye, quarreled. When General Yi was sent north against his will to fight the Ming armies, he raised the standard of revolt, returned and captured the Koryo capital of Songdo (now Kaesong). A story is told that one night during General Yi's campaign in the north he dreamed he was trying to rest while stretched over three logs. He was extremely uncomfortable. When he awoke he felt that his dream had possibly been a bad omen. He consulted Mu-hak Taesa, his favorite priest, who thoughtfully reassured him that the dream was a good sign. His body across the three logs formed the Chinese character for king (王). Indeed, he soon became the first Yi Dynasty king, but his rule certainly could not be considered a comfortable one with his many sons bickering for power.

At the age of fifty-eight, Yi Song-gye in 1392 became the king known as T'aejo and assumed the demanding duties of court reform. The emperor of China sent a message curtly asking how a man named Yi could become king without consent from Heaven (China). Matters were quickly explained and the new king diplomatically asked the emperor whether he preferred to call the new kingdom *choson* (Morning Freshness) or *hwaryung* (Peacefull Harmony). Hwaryung was another name of the city of Yonghung, birthplace of Yi Song-gye. Considering past events, it was obvious that there was little "peaceful harmony" in the kingdom, so the name Choson seemed more appropriate.

The name of Tumun-dong, a village located near the old Koryo capital of Songdo (Kaesong), is familiar to most Koreans because of the tragedy that took place here during the early years of the rule of Yi T'ae-jo. When the Koryo king had been overthrown and banished and the new Yi Dynasty was established, many leading scholars refused to recognize this presumptuous monarch. Though it was generally known that the Koryo government had been saturated with corruption, many government ministers felt that unquestioned loyalty must be given to the Koryo king and that abuses be dealt with internally. Seventy-seven of the country's leaders retired in protest to the town of Tumun-dong. King T'ae-jo repeatedly pleaded with them to forget a lost hope, come to the capital and help the new government build a better society for the nation. When the king's couriers arrived from Seoul, these scholars contemptuously refused to leave their homes to greet them. Sensing that stronger measures would be necessary to gain their cooperation, the king ordered their homes destroyed and the haughty scholars brought to the capital. He himself would then provide for them. The village was set afire and the king's officials waited in vain for the scholars to flee. This entire group of the educated elite chose to stay in their homes and die rather than submit to the will of the usurping king. Thus perished some of the finest scholars of that day; and King T'ae-jo was distraught, realizing that the opposition was far from reconciliation.

When any new dynasty comes into existence the problem of establishing a new capital must be settled. Originally it was decided to build the new capital at the foot of Kyeryong Mountain near Taejon City. Work commenced and even today foundation stones can be seen on the valley floor where the city planners had supervised construction. Consulting the records of ancient prophecy, it was found that Priest To-son, who had predicted the founding of the Koryo Dynasty, also had prophesied that the succeeding dynasty would build its capital at Hanyang (Seoul). This ninth century prophecy further asserted that the future dynasty of Yi would end in five hundred years, to be followed by a dynasty called Chong.

Legends tell of a young Korean girl whose husband died only a few weeks after their marriage. The young man was buried behind the house and over his grave grew miraculously a peach tree which bore one large fruit within the first year. Realizing that this peach must be special, the young girl and her father-in-law jealously guarded the fruit. However, one evening when the moon was full, the temptation became so great that the youthful widow plucked the supernatural fruit and ate it. She became pregnant and, when the villagers discovered her condition, she and her father-in-law were driven from the town. In due time in a lonely mountainous region she gave birth to a boy. After a few days a priest appeared, took the boy and disappeared into the mountains. The priest prophesied that the young boy would return and establish the Chong Dynasty with its capital at Kyeryong Mountain.

Priest Mu-hak traveled to Kyeryong Mountain where he was told to go to the area of present-day Seoul. There he instructed the city planners to build Kyongbok Palace to face Nam-san (South Mountain). However, the palace was built facing directly south rather than toward this mountain. "Very well," Mu-hak Taesa warned, "if you do not listen to me, you will

have cause to remember this mistake two hundred years from now."
Exactly two hundred years later, in 1592, the Japanese armies under Hideyoshi sacked Seoul and burned Kyongbok Palace to the ground.

Yi T'ae-jo is credited with having had an unusual vision in which a hen
swallowed a silkworm. No one could decipher the meaning until one
obscure court official (and he might have been a Chong) explained that
Kyeryong (Chicken Dragon) would swallow Chamdu. Kyeryong was
to be the site of a future dynastic capital according to Priest To-son's
prophecy, while Chamdu (Head of Silkworm) was the name of a spur
of South Mountain in Seoul City, capital of the new Yi Dynasty. Records
also noted that this poor official, somewhat deficient in discretion, paid
for his prophecy with his life.

This prophecy was partially fulfilled, in 1910, when Japan annexed Korea
and the occupation authorities called this new period Tae-chong (大鄭)
(Great Chong). However, no capital was constructed at Kyeryong Mountain, and today many descendants of the Chong family are still awaiting
their dynastic founder. They live in one of the few areas in modern Korea
where the topknot is still fashionable for married men, and where the
unmarried boy's hair is left to grow in a single braid.

One hundred years before Columbus discovered America, Yi T'ae-jo
broke ground for his magnificent Kyongbok Palace. A ten-mile wall
with nine city gates was constructed along the ridges of the encircling peaks,
and the court was moved from Songdo to make Seoul the country's capital.
Kyongbok Palace has been the setting for numerous court intrigues, beginning with those of King Yi T'ae-jo and ending with the murder of
Queen Min by the Japanese. King T'ae-jo's plan to name Prince Pang-suk
(son of his second wife, Queen Kang) his heir was frustrated by his ambiti-
ous fifth son T'ae-jong (by his first wife). Young T'ae-jong learned of his
father's plan and had his half brother Pang-suk and his friends slain. T'ae-jo
in a rage exiled himself to Hamhung. Later, in an unsuccessful attempt
at reconciliation near Tongduchon (north of Seoul), T'ae-jo angrily threw
the state seal at his wilful son.

Serving the Yi royal family for two hundred years, Kyongbok Palace
was burned during the Japanese invasion in the 25th year of Son-jo (14th
king). In the confusion of the invasion this splendid palace was actually
burned by Koreans.

In 1867, Kyongbok Palace was rebuilt by the regent Taewon-gun for
his second son Ko-jong, the young 26th king of Korea. In 1896, after Queen
Min's murder, King Ko-jong, accompanied by his son, was forced to flee
in a woman's palanquin to the Russian Legation. Remains of this once

dignified legation can be seen rising from a small hill behind Toksu Palace. After the Japanese annexed Korea in 1910, all but ten of the five hundred buildings that once formed Kyongbok Palace were torn down. A new capitol building was erected by the Japanese on the southern part of the palace grounds. The Japanese also moved the great South Gate of the palace to the east wall. In 1969, Kwanghwa Gate was reconstructed and returned to its original position. To further emphasize the government's interest in the use of the Korean phonetic alphabet, Korea's former President Park Chung-hee wrote the *han'gul* inscription over this gate..

The South Gate of Kyongbok Palace (Kwanghwa-mun) was moved to the east wall in 1926 to make way for the new capitol building seen behind. This building was used by the Japanese occupation government. The twin haet'ae *(fire-eating monsters) are still seen on each side of the gate after it was moved back to its original location in 1969. The Koreans now plan to turn this capitol building into the nation's National Museum.*

Kunjong-jon

Called the Hall of Government by Restraint, this building, which faced south down the main axis of the city, was the hub of T'ae-jo's capital. It was here that eight of the early Yi kings, beginning with Chong-jong (2nd king) and ending with Son-jo (14th king), were enthroned. Kunjong Gate had three doors opening onto the raised walkway leading to the great hall. As court officials entered, civilian dignitaries used the right walkway and military officials used the left side. The central portion is raised slightly higher and was used only by the monarch, who could not walk on the same level with his subjects. Stone markers on either side of the walkway denote the positions of the officials, with the highest rank being closest to the hall. The entire courtyard is paved with flagstones, making this audience hall truer to the original design than the other palaces. Around the courtyard twelve rusted iron rings are embedded firmly in the stone. Other rings are attached to the eaves of the audience hall. These were used for riggings which supported a canopy over a wide area of the courtyard.

Alongside the steps to the double-level platform, legendary *haet'ae* (fire-eating monsters) continue to protect the building from fire. On stone fence pillars, spaced symmetrically around the building, are the twelve animals of the zodiac and other mythical creatures.

In the center of the audience hall toward the rear is the king's throne. Behind the royal throne is a large painting depicting five peaks with pine trees and rivers flowing seaward. Two round circles at the top of either side of the painting represent the sun and moon, symbolic of west and east. The dragon design in the center of the ceiling indicates the presence of the king. This bright golden dragon is in bold relief and is well preserved.

Kunjong Gate

Directly behind the capitol is the impressive double-roofed gate which once let visitors into the courtyard of the Audience Throne Hall. Now hidden by the capitol this graceful structure must have been impressive when it stood directly in line between Kwanghwa-mun and Kunjong-jon. This large central gate flanked by two smaller gates now remains closed.

In winter beyond the audience hall of Kyongbok Palace courtiers heard the cry of pheasants. Now most of these stately structures of Yi have been destroyed and only the lonely wind sighs around the silent stones. Called Kunjong-jon (Hall of Government by Restraint), this building, which faced south down the main axis of the city, was the hub of T'ae-jo's capital.

Corridors Around Kunjong-jon

The historical treasures that are displayed in the side corridors of the audience hall are most interesting. There is a vast collection of plaques which once hung over historic gateways and buildings throughout the country. Most of the structures that the plaques identify no longer exist. A plaque located in the northeast corner is the original nameplate for the main gate of Toksu Palace. *taeahn-mun* (大安門) . The name was changed to *tae-han-mun* when Kojong made Toksu his royal retirement residence.

The images of Buddha come from various temples in Korea and are from the Koryo and Silla periods. One large metal Buddha, sitting on a pedestal and lacking its hands, is said to have once been covered with silver. The Japanese tried to move this image, but found it too heavy. They broke off the head, hoping to take at least this part, but couldn't move it. The head was again attached to the body. To make this image, the forms were cast in clay molds one section at a time and then pieced together. The seams are visible.

Also within the corridors stone tablets are displayed, and considered to be some of the oldest in the Orient. Lying near the stone carved inscriptions is a rusted cannon which was used by the French during the attack on Kanghwa Island in 1866. Also located here is a small tablet once located in Chongno which was written by the Taewon-gun. It states that to be friends with the foreigner is to sell out the country and it was the duty of every Korean to fight the Westerner.

One of Korea's oldest stone monuments is located in the eastern corridor. This tablet, one of five, was erected by King Chin-hung of Silla in 569 after the completion of his inspection tour. Until 1971 it stood on the peak of Pi-bong of north Seoul near Sungga-sa. The original site is still marked. The calligraphy is hardly legible but in the 18th century, Kim Chong-hi was able to translate as many of the characters as possible and carved his own translation into the side of the tablet.

He was able to decipher 68 characters of the original 150. Because of its great historical importance this 4.5 foot tablet is designated as National Treasure No. 3. The other four boundary stones are located, two in north Korea, one in Changyong Ṭown of South Kyongsang Province and one recently discovered in Paju-gun, north of Seoul.

Only two of three buildings, Sajong-jon and Ch'onch'u-jon, still remain directly north of the courtyard of the audience hall. The foundation on the right is all that is left of Manch'un-jon, which was destroyed during the Korean War. These buildings were used by government representatives, who would wait here for summoning if advice was needed.

Kwanghwa Gate

Kwanghwa Gate with its three arches and double-roofed pavilion was the most magnificent gate in the city and during the time of Yi kings it completely dominated the avenue leading to it. When the gate was originally built it soon collapsed. The geomancers were consulted and it was decided that the gate fell due to the influence of the crane. Therefore two towers were constructed on the southeast and southwest corner wall so as to anchor the wings of the crane. Tongshipcha-gak, the southeast tower, can still be seen separated from the wall and conspicuous in the whirl of traffic.

This South Gate of Kyongbok Palace was moved to the east wall to make way for the new capitol which was completed in 1926. When the communists retreated north in 1950, they burned the pavilion of this gate.

As a brutal reminder of the tragedies of war it remained for many years, until the gate was rebuilt in 1969 and moved back to its original location. The effect is naturally not the same with the capitol building behind it, but it is not altogether unpleasant. The new gate was made entirely of concrete rather than of wood; however, the restoration was skillfully accomplished.

Also in front of the capitol remain the twin *haet'ae*. It is claimed that this remarkable animal can tell right from wrong and is able to destroy evil, so has become a symbol of justice in China. The *haet'ae* also have the ability to eat fire and this was their main function as they once sat staring down the main avenue south from the palace.

Kyongbok Palace was plagued with frequent fires attributed to a spirit within a mountain south of the Han River called Kwanak-san, still superstitiously thought to be a potential volcano. To counteract this ill effect of Kwanak-san, Priest Mu-hak rebuilt and renamed Sammak Temple on the slope of the mountain and a copper dragon was dropped into the well near the temple. This served as a further protection against the ominous reputation of Mount Kwanak.

Kyonghoe-ru

This pavilion, smaller when first constructed during the reign of T'ae-jong (3rd king) in 1412, was named by the king's eldest son, Prince Yang-nyong, who inscribed the building's name on a plaque which can still be seen. Used for many purposes ranging from receptions for foreign envoys to national examinations, this hall was also the scene of the questionable court parties of the prodigal Yonsan-gun (10th king).

Because T'ae-jong wished to make his third son heir, Princes Yang-nyong and Hyo-nyong were passed over. It is said that Yang-nyong feigned irresponsibility and the second son became a priest to prevent dissension in the family over the selection of the third son. This third son became Se-jong, the greatest king of the Yi Dynasty.

Kyonghoe-ru was destroyed by the Japanese in 1592 but was restored in 1867 by the regent. It is interesting to notice that of the forty-eight pillars supporting this building, the inner ones are round and the other pillars square. This represents the Chinese concept of square shapes symbolizing earth and the round ones representing sky and space.

During the Korean War the building was damaged, but has been restored through funds from the American-Korean Foundation.

Chagyong-jon

The dowager Cho Shin-jong lived in Chagyong-jon until her death in 1890 at the age of eighty-one. She had married the crown prince, Ik-jong, when she was eleven and would have become queen if her husband had not died when he was twenty-one. When Sun-jo (23rd king) died in 1834, Cho's seven-year-old son became Hon-jong (24th king) and his grandmother Queen Kim became regent. Upon the death of Ch'ol-jong (25th king) in 1864, dowager Cho schemed with Hungson-gun in an attempt to put his second son on the Yi throne. Hungson-gun was the grandson of Unshin-gun, the son of Chang-jo (Prince Sa-do) by the concubine Yim Suk-bin. The plot succeeded. The powerful Andong Kim family was outwitted and Ko-jong (26th king) was placed on the throne when he was twelve years old. Hungson became the Taewon-gun and served as regent until Ko-jong came of age. Dowager Cho was like a mother to the young king, and lived out her days in this beautiful cluster of buildings.

On the inside and outside walls of the compound for Chagyong-jon are found some of the most interesting decorations in the brick construction. Plants, birds and animals are depicted in the brickwork. Behind the building on the inside wall is a complete scene called *ship-jang-saeng* which represents the ten long life symbols in Korea. (bamboo, rock, sun, cloud, pine, deer, water, turtle, crane and *pulloch'o*.)

Stone Memories of Religious Past

Along the walkway from Kyonghoe-ru to the former site of South Gate one can see many stone pagodas, lanterns and turtle tablets that were taken from major temples in Korea. This was done by the Japanese authorities in an attempt to beautify the grounds after the destruction of nearly all the palace buildings on these forty acres of land. Many of the pagodas and tablets date to Koryo and Silla periods and are listed as national treasures. From here, classic views of conical Pukak-san (North Mountain) rising majestically to the north may be seen, and to the left Inwang-san crouches like a wide wing-guard for the palace. The city wall like a winding snake can be glimpsed on the ridges of these peaks.

Site of Sujong-jon

South of the impressive Kyonghoe-ru and its lotus pond is a small building on the site of Sujong-jon. This building once housed a folklore museum which was later moved to a larger building in the northern section of the

On the palace walls numerous designs representing "long life" and "good luck" symbols and patterns, including the ship-jang-saeng, can be seen pleasantly arranged between the brick motif.

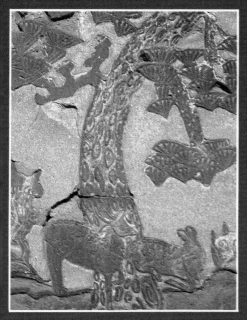

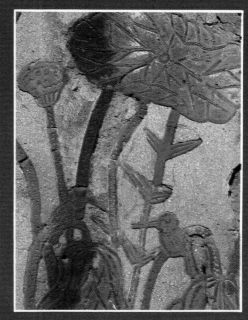

palace grounds. Sujong-jon was the structure which housed Se-jong's (4th king) former library and it is believed that it was within this building that scholars developed the Korean alphabet or *han'gul* during the early fifteenth century. The king appointed a group of scholars to develop an alphabet so that the lower classes might be provided with books they could read in their own language. Prior to this all literature was in Chinese. Though appreciated by the masses, the new alphabet offended many of the ranking scholars, who thought the classics were being "dragged in the dust" by becoming available to the people. During the period of weak kings and strong court officials, *han'gul* was relegated to less importance and finally not used. As a result of the efforts of the first Christian missionaries to Korea, *han'gul* was brought out of disuse to become the common written language. The development of the *han'gul* is considered one of Korea's greatest achievements.

Hamhwa-dang

This building was originally used as an audience hall for foreigners. The eaves are decorated with water lily blooms and seven-character poems are inscribed on hanging wooden plaques.

Hyangwon Pavilion

This area with a lotus pond was constructed by King Ko-jong in 1868 as a place to stroll and meditate during leisure hours. Hyangwon (Far Reaching Fragrance) Pavilion is an appropriate name, since it is situated on an island. The original bridge spanned the pond from the pavilion to Konch'ong Palace to the north. During the communist invasion this bridge was destroyed; as a convenience to visitors it was later reconstructed across the southern portion of the pond. In the spring, summer, fall or winter this bridge and pavilion have unique charm and innate beauty which photographers and painters often attempt to capture.

Chipok-jae and P'algak-jong

Built in 1867 by King Ko-jong as an auxiliary structure to the royal residence, Chipok-jae was used as a personal library. This library is in the traditional Chinese architecture, whereas the building to the left is Korean. The Chinese name plaques read from top to bottom, and the Korean ones usually from right to left. Atop each end of the roof ridge is a bronze dragon signifying that royalty used this building. Colorful flowers, including water lily and plum blossoms, decorate the eaves of both build-

Fragrance Pavilion

Probably the most famous of pavilions in Seoul's palaces is the Hyangwon Pavilion (Far Reaching Fragrance) located south of Konch'ong Palace where Queen Min was murdered in 1895. Beyond the pavilion is the National Folklore Museum on the site of the Konch'ong Palace which was destroyed by the Japanese. Posing for a photograph by the Pavilion of Far Reaching Frangrance is the most popular thing to do on a Sunday afternoon.

ings. The stone *haet'ae* used as guard-rails are to protect the building from destruction. To the left of the library is an octagonal pavilion called P'algak, used for the king's collection of rare books. After the Korean War it was found that the north Korean communists had carried off most of the more valuable editions. Until early 1968 people could freely enter the grounds; however, they are now off limits to the general public. Since the infiltration of 1968 and assassination attempt upon the president, military guards have been posted. The North Gate of Kyongbok Palace is adjacent to the presidential home, and through the trees the blue tiles of the Blue House can be seen.

The Former Kangnyong-jon and Kyot'ae-jon

In two buildings forming the center of Kyongbok Palace lived the king and queen. In 1919, the year that King Ko-jong died, these buildings were removed to Ch'angdok Palace and the grounds ceased to exhibit the traditional architecture of a king's palace. Remnants of the once splendid royal gardens can be seen. Pines, pavilions, man-made hills, streams and bridges for the most part have vanished. Now the larger trees provide the curious tourist with a pleasant, shady place to rest on hot summer days. Compared with Ch'angdok Palace, Kyongbok Palace has lost its regal grandeur; nevertheless the spirit of a country's rich culture and proud achievements can be sensed in the remains of this greatest of Yi Dynasty palaces. One marvels at the vision that the first king of the dynasty had over five hundred years ago.

National Folklore Museum

Korea's first private folklore museum began after liberation in 1945. In 1966 under the sponsorship of the Cultural Property Preservation Bureau of the Ministry of Culture and Information a small museum opened at Sujong-jon in Kyongbok Palace opposite Kyonghoe-ru. However, after the opening of the new National Museum, the National Art Gallery was moved to make way for the National Folklore Museum which opened in April 1975.

Nine galleries are used which depict in an excellent manner all aspects of early Korean life. Traditional farming methods, hunting, weaving, cooking and other housekeeping chores are portrayed. Religious rituals including shaman, Buddhist and Confucian ceremonies are vividly portrayed by manikins. Other areas of commerce and industry pursued during the Yi Dynasty are delineated in a pleasing manner.

In the area of handicrafts the displays include pottery making, woodcraft, lacquerware, hats, baskets, mats and tools of the trade or instruments for pleasure. The sophisticated workmanship is often indigenous to Korea and portrays genre characteristics. Special notice should be given to the paper making and sericulture industry. The quality of work was recognized throughout the Orient.

A traditional *yangban* (nobleman's) house was brought from Andong and reconstructed within one gallery. The various rooms of this aristocratic home are seen with typical furniture used. The architectural techniques include the joining of pillars and brackets in an interlocking manner which is almost forgotten in modern Korea.

Also of interest to the curious foreigner is the vast display of Korean type clothing seldom seen now. These include a wide variety of hats, shoes, women's ornaments for clothing and hair. Embroidered emblems which distinguish rank and position are portrayed by animals and birds.

A typical wedding scene, a hundred-day ceremony for a baby and a *hwan'gap* (sixtieth birthday) celebration are all well illustrated by life-size figures.

Ancestor worship, shaman rituals and mask dance drama, using the traditional musical instruments, are given their due recognition in Korea's fascinating folklore tradition. Films are also shown on a regular basis in an auditorium.

The National Folklore Museum is north of Hyangwon Pavilion and on the site of Konch'ong Palace and Konnyong-gak, private living quarters of King Ko-jong and Queen Min. In 1893 a pseudo-religious movement called Tonghak started a revolt in south Korea and developed into a revolutionary reform crusade, professing loyalty to the king but opposition to existing corruption in the government. Chinese troops were called in by the government to put down this movement. Because the advance notification required by the Sino-Japanese agreement of 1885 was not observed, Japanese troops also moved into the capital and were victorious in the war. The treaty that followed provided for Korean independence. A Japanese minister, Count Inouye, was sent to Seoul to help institute reforms which did not satisfy the people because of their origin.

Count Inouye was replaced by Count Miura, who felt that Queen Min was the greatest obstacle to the accomplishment of Japanese objectives in Korea. The Taewon-gun (former regent), living in retirement, allied himself with the Japanese against his daughter-in-law. It has been rumored that one of the queen's personal servants, a girl who was referred to by the Japanese name of "Hanako," agreed to further the plot by identifying the queen to the soldiers. A message was slipped out of the palace saying that her forehead would be marked with red to identify her as the informant. On October 8, 1895, soldiers stormed into the palace and "Hanako" disguised as a *sanggung* (court lady) pointed out the room where the queen was hiding. After killing the queen, the soldiers dragged her body to Nok-san (Deer Mountain), the hill just east of her residence, where they poured fuel on it and burned it.

After Korea's annexation in 1910, the place and private living quarters were torn down by the Japanese. In Ch'angdok Palace there is a picture of the original buildings. This building was constructed by the Japanese. Though damaged during the Korean War it was restored. For many years it served as a National Art Gallery. From 1975 it has been used as the National Folklore Museum.

After studying old records, historians have pinpointed the actual place where Queen Min was murdered. A three-step platform with a monument inscribed with Queen Min's name and title can be seen to the right of the museum. Dr. Syngman Rhee, former president of the Republic of Korea, wrote the inscription and dedicated this site on June 6, 1954. The monument and the wooded area to the east stand as a grim reminder of a tragic moment in Korean history.

The National Folklore Museum is open daily from 10–5 PM except Sundays and legal holidays. To enter one must first buy an entrance ticket to Kyongbok Palace and there is a small additional charge to enter the museum. It is not necessary to go through the National Museum grounds but one must walk from Konch'un Gate through Kyongbok Palace to the far north wall.

Korea's National Museum

The National Museum of Korea, located on the grounds of Kyongbok Palace, preserves over 90,000 artifacts of historical and archaeological importance. Now branch museums of the National Museum are located in Kyongju, Puyo, Kongju and Kwangju.

The beginnings of early museum development in Korea started during the Japanese occupation in 1915 when a small collection of Korean treasures were placed on exhibit in Kyongbok Palace. However, until 1945 the Japanese authorities had complete control and many of Korea's priceless treasures were taken to Japan, never to be returned.

After liberation the known Korean collection was turned over to Kim Jae-won, the senior statesman for museum development. This collection totalled about 13,000 articles. Within five years the collection grew to 20,000 but the outbreak of the Korean War placed these treasures in jeopardy.

Fortunately when Seoul was recaptured most of the treasures were found intact in the basement of the Museum of Modern Art in the Toksu Palace. When the Chinese armies threatened to invade Seoul, the entire collection was moved to Pusan.

From 1955 the collection was housed in the Museum of Modern Art in the Toksu Palace until a new museum could be constructed in Kyongbok Palace. This permanent Museum building was completed in 1972.

The architecture of the National Museum building is a type of monument recognizing Korea's cultural past. The architectural design is a replica of the national treasures located at Popehu-sa, Hwaom-sa and Kumsan-sa.

In the nine halls a complete spectrum of 5000 years of Korean art can be viewed, including prehistoric artifacts, excavated tomb ornaments, Buddhist relics, outstanding earthenware, stoneware, celadon and porcelain, as well as paintings and bronzes.

Neolithic remains excavated at Amsa-dong in Seoul date to 3000 BC and represent some of Korea's oldest artifacts. Early bronzes dating to 300 BC portray Shamanistic characteristics. One of Korea's most spectacular tomb excavations (Tumulus No. 155) took place in 1973 in Kyongju, the old Silla capital. The gold crown with other articles are on display dating to the fifth century era.

The craftsmanship of 8th century bronze reveals a rich Buddhist culture and many examples are seen. A large Maitreya Buddha, 37 inches high, is exhibited in a sitting position with one hand touching the chin as if thinking. Most of the exhibits have been discovered following the Korean War.

In the pottery collection is a wide variety of ceramics from pre-history through early Silla to the exquisite masterpieces of the Koryo dynasty's celadons. The uniqueness of *punch'ong* pottery which represents Korea's genre art is presented with simplicity and good taste. Porcelains from the Yi Dynasty period are plain white or with cobalt blue, coppered or iron black designs and possess a mystic capability for impressing the visitor with a deeper understanding of the creative genius of the Korean potter.

Masterpieces of Yi Dynasty paintings include An Kyon, Yun Tu-so, Shim Sa-jong, Yi In-mun, Kim Hong-do, Shin Yun-bok and many others. During this Confucian period the painting style rapidly developed following Chinese patterns; however, genre painting did reveal itself. Though the mainstream was orthodox paintings during the Yi Dynasty, the folk and Buddhist paintings continued to flourish and today bring high prices in the antique market.

Mr. Han Byong Sam is the present director of the National Museum. On his staff he has many assistants who are extremely capable and speak excellent English. Mr. Han Chol-mo is director of the International Department and Chung Yang-moo is chief curator.

When the dramatic exhibition of *5000 Years of Korean Art* opened in the Asian Art Museum of San Francisco on May 1, 1979 to begin a two year tour of the US, a new awareness of Korea's art heritage was vividly portrayed to the Western world. The days of taking a "back seat" to the arts of Japan and China are over. However, in Korea the development of adequate display technology still needs to be encouraged. As foreign tourists increase in number, adequate written information and tape guides need to be produced so that visitors do not walk away discouraged.

At present detailed information in English is almost non-existent. If you wish to make your museum tour a true learning experience, take with you a guide who knows the subject. Possibly the impetus created by the *5000 Years of Korean Art* will motivate Korean museum authorities to rejuvenate the presentation of Korean antiquity, culture and art for the interested foreign public.

The National Museum is open daily from 10—5:00 except Monday and legal holidays. The National Museum has a separate gate and entrance fee other than the one for Kyongbok Palace.

East Gate of Kyongbok

The visitor today would enter usually through this East Gate of the Kyongbok Palace. The gentle curve of the tile roof with the clay *chapsang* silhouetted against the clear blue sky makes this gate an excellent backdrop for taking photographs of the picturesque 13-storied pagoda directly inside.

Other Palace Gates

Around the walls of Kyongbok Palace were four main gates. The main South Gate, Kwanghwa-mun, and East Gate, Konch'un-mun, have already been mentioned. In Chinese cosmology there is assigned to each of the four directions an element and virtue as well as a season and divinity. Therefore, east is associated with the blue dragon and spring. The name of the East Gate of Kyongbok means "establishing spring." The northern direction is associated with winter and the divine black warriors and the west with autumn and the white tiger. The North Gate is called Shinmu-mun or Gate of Divine Warriors while the West Gate or Yongch'u-mun means "welcoming autumn." The southern direction relates to summer and the red bird.

During the Yi Dynasty the East Gate was used by royal relatives and court officials while the North Gate was opened only for the king himself. The North Gate because of its proximity to the presidential Blue House is tightly secured and not used by the general public. The West Gate which was demolished when the capitol was built was used to admit people on general court business. The West Gate was recently reconstructed along the western wall near the building which houses the Cultural Property Preservation Office of the Ministry of Culture and Information. The West Gate is also not open to the general public.

CH'ILGUNG SHRINE
(Memorial to Seven Concubines)

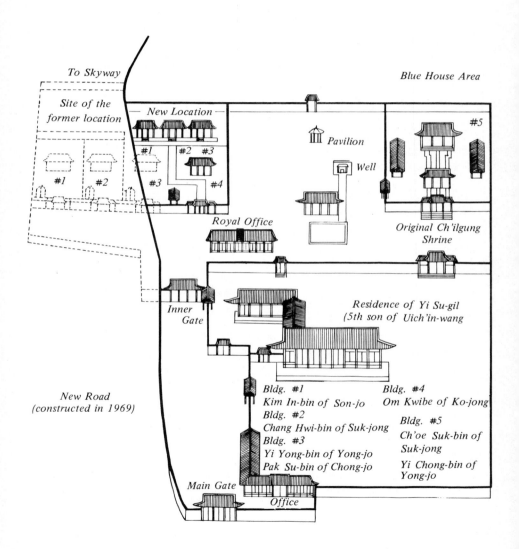

To Skyway

Blue House Area

Site of the former location

New Location

Pavilion

Well

#5

#1
#2 #3
#3 #4

#1
#2
#3

Royal Office

Original Ch'ilgung Shrine

Inner Gate

Residence of Yi Su-gil (5th son of Uich'in-wang

New Road (constructed in 1969)

Bldg. #1
Kim In-bin of Son-jo
Bldg. #2
Chang Hwi-bin of Suk-jong
Bldg. #3
Yi Yong-bin of Yong-jo
Pak Su-bin of Chong-jo

Bldg. #4
Om Kwibe of Ko-jong

Bldg. #5
Ch'oe Suk-bin of Suk-jong
Yi Chong-bin of Yong-jo

Main Gate

Office

Ch'ilgung (Shrine of the Seven Palaces)

(Located northwest of Kyongbok Palace)

This unusual shrine was first constructed as a memorial for concubine Ch'oe in 1725, shortly after Yong-jo (21st Yi king) came to the throne. Ch'oe Suk-bin was one of the numerous concubines of Suk-jong (19th king) and died in 1718 two years before her husband. She became important posthumously when her son became the twenty-first king.

After 1908, six other concubines' memorial tablets were moved to this area and additional shrine buildings were constructed. All seven concubines had the distinction of having their sons named to be kings. One was made a king posthumously and two others did not live long enough to rule. In front of the shrine area is the private home of Yi Su-gil, fifth son of Uich'in-wang (son of King Ko-jong).

The process of modernization has again taken its toll on a cultural site, as a city road was constructed through the beautiful grounds of Ch'ilgung Shrine. As a result, in 1969 the first three buildings were torn down and relocated behind the other buildings. Also because of its close proximity to the Presidential Home (Blue House) this shrine is not open to the general public. Actually a stone's-throw away is the site of the 1979 presidential assassination of Park Chung-hee.

Possibly in the future the doors will be opened and the public will be enthralled by the most enchanting shrine in Seoul.

Shrine No. 1: (Building moved)

Kim In-bin was a concubine of Son-jo (14th king) and the mother of Won-jong, who was raised to royal status after his death. The family line was becoming extremely weak during this period. Won-jong was the father of King In-jo (16th king), who wrested the throne from the irresponsible Kwanghae-gun.

Shrine No. 2: (Building moved)

This shrine memorializes the infamous concubine Chang Hui-bin, who created jealous friction between Suk-jong (19th king) and his second queen, Queen Min, who was spurned but was later reinstated. Chang's continued scheming proved to be her undoing and she was sentenced to die by poison. Chang was the mother of Kyong-jong, who in 1720 became the short-lived twentieth Yi king.

In winter beyond the audience hall of Injong-jon one can still hear the cry of pheasants. Silent beauty sparkles each season lending charm in Ch'angdok Palace. Occasionally the chatter of voices of palace visitors disturbs the calm of brick-patterned walls leading through gates into courtyards beyond and to the secret gardens of Kajong-dang.

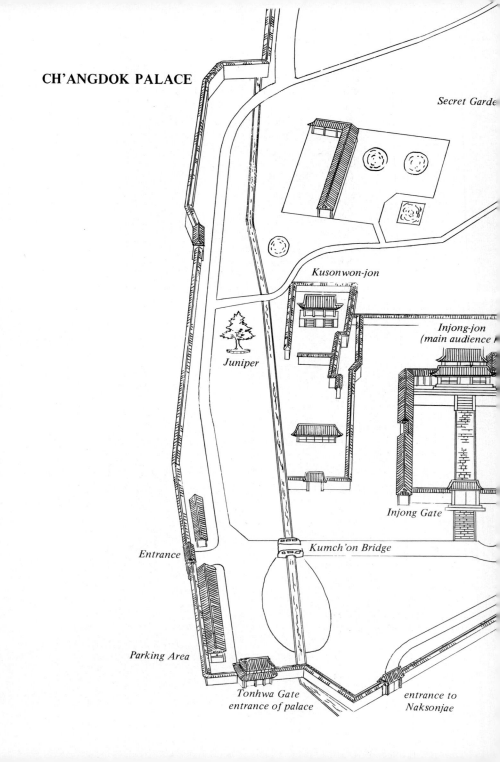

CH'ANGDOK PALACE

Secret Garde

Kusonwon-jon

*Injong-jon
(main audience*

Juniper

Injong Gate

Entrance

Kumch'on Bridge

Parking Area

*Tonhwa Gate
entrance of palace*

*entrance to
Naksonjae*

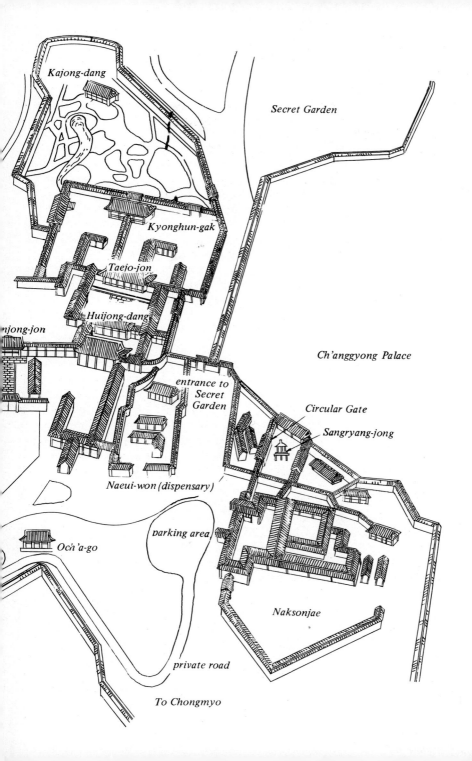

Kajong-dang

Secret Garden

Kyonghun-gak

Taejo-jon

Huijong-dang

jong-jon

Ch'anggyong Palace

entrance to
Secret
Garden

Circular Gate

Sangryang-jong

Naeui-won (dispensary)

parking area

Och'a-go

Naksonjae

private road

To Chongmyo

Tonhwa-mun

As one enters the south palace gate, leaving the turbulent city behind, one slips into the realm of Yi Dynasty history. The tranquility of a royal court pervades the mind. Massive trees, attempting to stretch their aging limbs across the wide path, grow beside this towering gate, which may have already thrown its afternoon shadow into the nearby rose garden. Tonhwa Gate with its five entrance openings is possibly the most famous wooden structure of the early Yi Dynasty period remaining in Seoul. The central entrance was used only by the king. As the court dignitaries entered, civilian officials used the right gate and military officials the left. The right side (east) always held more honor than the left side (west), and in time of war the positions were reserved, with the military taking the honored side.

A most bizarre episode took place in front of this gate during the reign of Yong-jo (21st king). Yi Chong-sung, a faithful minister of the king, heard of a plot that upset him greatly and, despising the constant squabble of party feuds which a few years before had caused the king to murder his own son, Yi Chong-sung took his fishing pole and went to the Han River to mediate. Into the silvery waters that flowed past the capital the elderly statesman dropped his line and concentrated on the distant horizen.

While he was thus deep in thought a young man from the south approached the motionless scholar. After the young man introduced himself, the old man discovered that the traveler had come to Seoul to seek his fortune. The young man hesitantly inquired if the elderly grandfather knew of someone who could help him find a position. Yi Chong-sung gave the young man an address and told him to go to that house. The next day the man did so and discovered that the house belonged to Yi Chong-sung, the scholar he had met at the river's bank. Two days later he was made chief guard of Tonhwa Gate and, since being unfamiliar with the faces of the different palace attendants, carefully scrutinized everyone. Yi Chong-sung noted his conscientious spirit with a sense of deep satisfaction.

Shortly afterwards a *nain* (personal maid) whom the young guard had seen before approached Tonhwa Gate at a late hour carrying a food box. The slender girl appeared to be in a great hurry, and for a moment he wondered whether he should take the time to detain her. Yet he had a duty to perform, so, stepping out into the cool air, he asked to see the contents of the box. The startled girl was first annoyed and then angry at this delay. "It is only food for my mistress, the concubine Mun, who is about to give birth to the new heir of Yi," snapped the maid. She tried to brush past but the guard stood firm. "When my mistress hears of this she'll have your head on a pole before mid-day tomorrow," threatened the girl. "I will not be killed for doing my duty," shouted the young guard, as he became angrier. The girl, he thought, was being very stubborn about an insignificant thing. Finally in an uncontrolled rage the girl threw herself against the guard in an attempt to dash into the palace. Convinced that something was wrong, he drew his sword and slashed the box. There was a sudden cry and blood spurted from the food box. The girl broke into tears, and as the guard opened the box a dead baby was exposed.

Strange shades of intrigue suddenly came to light on this dark night as the baby's blood oozed into the ground in front of Tonhwa-mun. Mun So-ui, concubine of Yong-jo, had pretended for nine months to be with child. Plotting with others, she assisted in having Sa-do Seja, the crown prince, condemned to die through false accusations. Placed in a rice box in front of a small gate in Ch'anggyong Palace, he had suffocated in 1762. Now the concubine Mun was attempting to smuggle into Ch'angdok Palace a baby boy who would be made heir and possibly king of Korea. Her most trusted personal maid had been sent to the village for this child, and, if she had returned successfully to the concubine with the boy, she would have been rewarded with death. No one would then knew of the deception. Somehow Yi Chong-sung knew of this plot, yet did not know how to expose it. After solving this case, he retired. Concubine Mun was killed and the son of Sa-do Seja became king in 1776. King Yong-jo loved Yi Chong-sung so much that at his tomb he wrote about this old man who took his fishing pole and sat in the hot summer sun for him.

a sitting man, Sam-jong Popsa, a priest of early China who was later deified. A monkey, pig, snake and other creatures are further back. On the ridge crest is the dragon head representing royalty which is used only on buildings that might be occupied by the king. Along the central ridge five ornate plum blossoms can be seen. The Chinese characters for "Yi" and Damson Plum are the same, thus the dynasty's crest. The five blossoms might represent the five hundred years of the dynasty's existence as prophesied by the Silla priest, To-son Kuksa. Sometime before 1392, a Koryo king came to this area and planted many plum trees, only to have them mutilated several years later. This was done in an attempt to delay and forestall the prophetic rise of a new Yi Dynasty. Obviously the plan failed.

Originally the structure was painted predominantly in red and green, the colors used by kings, but in the year that King Ko-jong declared Korea's independence from China the color scheme was changed to yellow, the imperial color of the Emperor of Heaven.

The hall itself has a high elegantly painted and gilded ceiling supported by numerous great red pillars. During the Japanese occupation, major changes were made in this throne room. Electric lights were installed and curtains were added. The throne chair was also altered, but in 1964 repairs were made to restore this hall as near to the original as possible. However, the audience hall at Kyongbok Palace is still the most authentic.

Behind the throne seat is a large screen which depicts the adopted Confucian symbolism. As one faces the throne, the sun seen on the left is the *yang* (the king's right), while the moon on the right represents the weaker force *um* (the king's left). Again the number five is symbolically represented in five mountain peaks; these peaks may be the "Five Happinesses" or the five elements of wood, fire, earth, metal and water. One authority states that the four points of the compass are represented with the king's peak in the center. Water flows continually from the five peaks and illustrates the long-life desire; the evergreen pine has the same significance. The coronation ceremonies of seven of the later dynasty kings were held in this hall. The entire courtyard was seeded with grass during the Japanese occupation, although traditionally grass was grown only at burial sites. Thus the elimination of the flagstones in this courtyard was a departure from authenticity.

Within the throne room of Ch'angdok Palace a screen, rich in Confucian symbolism, always stood behind the throne. As one faces the throne the left circle is the sun (or yang*) and position of the king. The right side is moon (or* um*), the position of the queen. The five peaks are the "Five Happinesses" or five elements and five compass directions, (Center direction symbolizes the king).*

Corridors Around Injong-jon

Along the corridors on both sides of the main courtyard of Injong-jon are several reception rooms which at one time housed a small museum of royal articles. Once many rare portraits of Yi Dynasty rulers were on display here. During the Korean War they were taken to Pusan for safe-keeping but through an accidental fire all but four of them were burned. Three were badly charred and the one left unscathed was of Yong-jo (21st king). (He ruled the longest of any Yi kings.) The museum was closed in 1978 and all the royal household effects and gallery of early photographs of royal family members are in storage at Ch'angdok Palace. A large blue cloisonne incense urn presented by the Chinese to Emperor Ko-jong is still seen in the entryway to the corridors.

Sonjong-jon

East of the main throne hall is this small audience chamber, once used for receiving civil and military officials and, later, foreign dignitaries. Sonjong-jon was rebuilt in 1653 during the reign of Hyo-jong (17th king). This is the only building now roofed with blue glazed tiles. It is claimed

that before the Hideyoshi invasion most palace roofs were covered with blue tiles. This ceramic technique which had been developed during the Koryo Dynasty at Kaesong was lost. Yi Dynasty artisans attempted to reproduce this blue tile, but eventually realized that their efforts were futile and abandoned the project.

An interesting architectural effect can be observed from the courtyard in front of Sonjong-Jon. Looking back at the roofs of Injong-jon, one notices that the roof tiles appear to be the same size. Actually, the farther ones are larger. If the roof tiles were all the same size the farther ones would seem smaller, thus making the main audience hall more insignificant than the building in the foreground.

Huijong-dang

In the residential portion of the palace one finds a series of semi-European style reception rooms with carpeting, mirrors and upholstered chairs which were imported from France and used in the palace renovation for Sun-jong (27th king). Also admirable is the Chinese-style furniture. This palace, rebuilt in 1615, served the kings as an informal place for managing the affairs of state. Before the completion of the new Kyongbok Palace, the dowager Queen Cho (wife of Ik-jong) and the regent Taewon-gun used these rooms for formulating the policies of Korea during the teen-age years of King Ko-jong. The former royal residence of Kangnyong-jon, once located in the Kyongbok Palace, was moved to this site in 1920. On the eastern wall is a room-wide mural of the Diamond Mountains of northern Korea as seen from the sea. For contrast, on the opposite wall these same mountains are depicted viewed from the land. Considered one of the scenic wonders of the world, the southern palisade of pinnacles extends to Sorak Mountain near Sokcho on the east coast.

Taejo-jon

Descending the steps from Huijong-dang and then entering an inner gate, one reaches a small courtyard directly in front of the private living quarters of the king and his family. During the Japanese occupation, when Kyongbok Palace was being dismantled, Kyot'ae Hall was moved to this site and renamed Taejo-jon, the original name of the buildings that had been destroyed by fire. A small locked gate on the left leads to the palace kitchen. The series of rooms beginning from the left were the bathroom, queen's bedroom, living room and private room for the crown prince.

Naksonjae

Behind the walls of Naksonjae (Mansion of Joy and Goodness), Yi Dynasty history has come to a slow halt. The few remaining occupants of these rooms are the living links between the modern progressive Republic of Korea and the impressive Yi Dynasty period which has left its indelible mark on history. Down these rambling corridors the silent echoes are almost oppressive, yet in the picturesque gardens of forsythia, azalea and blooming cherry trees, birds still chatter among the eaves of pavilions and gates joining the three palace courts of Naksonjae. These private quarters at Naksonjae are not open to the general public, so special permission to visit them must be obtained. In 1979 a private entrance to Naksonjae was made east of the main gate, Tonhwa-mun.

Until a few years ago three old and fragile *sanggung* (court ladies) could be seen slipping in and out of Naksonjae's gate. On October 24, 1968, their duties officially ended as the *wip'ae* (spirit tablet) of Queen Yun, last queen and second wife of King Sun-jong, was placed with ceremonious ritual in the Chongmyo Shrine. In 1977 the three court ladies moved to private homes in the city. Kim Myong-gil, the eldest of the three, began her training when she was thirteen. She was given the title of Escorting *Sanggung* when Queen Yun entered the palace as a bride of twelve in 1906. Pak Chang-bo, who is now seventy-six, also entered the service of the royal family at the age of thirteen. The youngest is Sanggung Song, who is now sixty. Only Sanggung Kim entered the palace prior to the close of the dynasty in 1910.

When Queen Yun died in February 1966 and was buried next to her husband at Kumgok, her memorial spirit tablet was brought to Naksonjae and placed behind an altar. It then became the duty of the *sanggung* to serve the spirit of Queen Yun as they had faithfully served her while she was alive. They prepared daily food and promptly at 8:00 a.m. and 5:00 p.m. placed it before the shrine during the entire mourning period. At 9:00 p.m. on February 10, 1968, the final ritual of the mourning period was held in Naksonjae, and conducted by Yi Ku with other members of the Yi Dynasty Relatives Association participating. Though the official period of grief was over, the tablet remained in Naksonjae until October and then was solemnly placed in the cubicle reserved for Queen Yun's tablet to the right of King Sun-jong's in the shrine called Chongmyo. The doors of the shrine were opened for the first time since 1945. Ceremonial recognition and prayers for the spirits of the kings and queens of the Yi Dynasty were offered.

Naksonjae

*Drifting noiselessly, down
  through the trees,
As if bringing a message
  from above,
Like a slice of a forgotten
  memory.
I sit quietly in a somber
  garb
And my nostalgia slowly
  settles
Upon the snow piling up
  endlessly.
A lantern burns low under
  the eaves,
As I stroll alone into the
  palace gardens.*

Naksonjae was first constructed in 1846 by order of Hon-jong (24th king) for his concubine, Kim Kyong-bin. She was fourteen years old at the time. King Hon-jong had married his second queen two years before, after the death of fifteen-year-old Queen Kim. Queen Hong was only thirteen and evidently the king was not overly infatuated with her, since Naksonjae was constructed for the concubine Kim. The only child that King Hon-jong had was by another concubine, Kim Suk-ui. This daughter died in her early years and was buried at So-sam-nung.

During this period King Hon-jong was still in his teens and the country was administered by the regent, dowager Queen Kim (wife of King Sun-jo). Though King Hon-jong died at twenty-two in 1849, his concubine lived to the age of seventy-six and died in 1908.

Naksonjae continued to be used by the later queens of the Yi Dynasty, and Queen Yun, Sun-jong's wife and the last queen of the monarchy, moved into these rooms upon the death of her husband in 1926. Except for short periods during the Korean War and the latter part of the First Republic, Naksonjae was Queen Yun's official residence. After the revolution she again asked permission to return, and remained in Naksonjae until her death.

Queen Yun was born in Myongdong, Seoul. Her older brother studied in the United States and obtained a doctor's degree. She also had one younger brother and one younger sister. This sister married Yu Ok-kyom who became Education Minister and president of Yonsei University. Yun (Sun-jong) was recommended to Om Kwibi (wife of Ko-jong) by her father's elder brother, who was Sun-jong's private secretary. Following through on this suggestion, the queen had the girl's name placed on a list with other equally well-qualified girls. After a three-step elimination, which included interviews and thorough evaluation of educational background, family heritage and beauty, the intellectual and poised Yun (Sun-jong) was chosen.

Then followed the normal thirty-day period of intensive instruction, during which time the future bride learned court protocol and the practical feminine art of how to woo a husband and king as well as his parents. The future queen completed the course in only twenty days. On a December day in 1906 the wedding was held with all its regal celebration. The couple moved into Toksu Palace and a year later, when Ko-jong retired, moved to Ch'angdok Palace. They had no children.

Queen Yun possessed an unusual aptitude for languages, being fluent in Chinese, Japanese and English. Also having a musical talent, she studied piano and voice.

The tragic story of the heroic hardships she bore during the Korean War portrayed the brave and courageous spirit of this gentle woman. She was permitted to return to Naksonjae in 1960 and often received visitors during her final six years of life.

Also living at Naksonjae in quiet seclusion is Princess Tok-hye, the only living child of a Korean king, daughter of King Ko-jong's seventh wife, Yang Pongyong-dang. Princess Tok-hye was born in 1912. Forced to marry a Japanese aristocrat in 1928, she had one daughter who died following World War II. After liberation she was given permission to return to Korea and now at the age of seventy has found a place of peace for her remaining years.

The addition in front of Naksonjae was built by the Japanese in 1927 and is now the official home of Princess Pang-ja (Masako), the mother of Kyu Lee (Yi Ku) and wife of the last crown prince of Korea, Yi Un. The story of this amazing woman is told in her autobiography *The World is One,* in which she relates how as a Japanese princess she woke up one morning to read in the papers that she was to marry a Korean prince. She had also been recently considered as a possible selection for the young crown prince of Japan, Hirohito.

Young Princess Masako's personal happiness was sacrificed for political expediency and she was powerless to resist. Born of noble lineage and considered as a possible bride for Japan's crown prince, suddenly she found herself at the age of nineteen plunged into the maelstrom of political intrigue.

Her husband was Yongch'in-wang (Yi Un), younger half-brother to King Sun-jong who had abdicated a decade before. Their first child, Yi Chin, died tragically and suddenly on a state visit from Japan to Korea in 1922. Some think he was actually poisoned. Their second son Kyu was born and educated in Japan. In 1950 he departed for the United States where he completed his master's degree in architecture at MIT, eventually became a naturalized US citizen, and married Miss Julia Mullock.

The paramount desire of Kyu Lee's father, Yongch'in-wang, was to return to Korea, his homeland. Though the dynasty had ended he had been given the title of Crown Prince because King Sun-jong had no children. So Kyu Lee as heir to the dynasty follows the prophetic tradition that Yi Dynasty successions would be through a second or younger son of the king. He never actually expected to return to the land of his heritage. But in 1963 the Korean government gave permission for Yi Un (Yongch'in-wang) to come to Korea with his family. Naksonjae was remodeled for the family's homecoming.

Tragically, Yongch'in-wang returned to his homeland too late. He was an invalid and had to be confined to the hospital for the next seven years. A few hours before his death on May 1, 1970 the Crown Prince was taken to Naksonjae. He and his wife had celebrated their fiftieth wedding anniversary only two days before. Yongch'in-wang's spirit tablet is now enshrined in Chongmyo.

After their arrival to Korea, Kyu Lee and his wife Julia adopted Eugenia, a Korean orphan. She recently graduated from a university in the US. Kyu Lee (Yi Ku) continues to serve as titular head of the Yi Dynasty Association.

At the age of eighty-two when most people are enjoying retirement Princess Pang-ja is still active in promoting vocational education among the the physically handicapped of her adopted country in *Myonghui-won*, an association she started. In 1972 the Korean government conferred the Order of National Merit on her for her achievements.

Bottom: This recent photograph taken on July 24, 1971 in Tokyo represents the blend of royalty from Japan to Korea. Sitting is Itsuko Nashimoto, wife of Prince Morimasa Nashimoto. Sitting to her right is Princess Masako (Yi Pang-ja), her daughter and wife of the Korean crown prince Yi Un. Standing is her second son Yi Ku (Mr. Kyu Lee) and Julia. Standing between is Eugenia, their Korean adopted daughter.

Right Page: Yi Un (Yongch'in-wang) was the last crown prince of the Yi Dynasty. This official photograph of Yongch'in-wang was taken in 1935 when he was a regimental commander in the Uchinomiya District of Tokyo. In 1963 he returned to Korea and on May 1, 1970, quietly passed away at Naksonjae at the age of seventy-three. (Princess Yi Pang-ja's private collection)

李　垠

Top Right: *Visitors to Ch'ang-dok Palace stop to read the notice of the death of Prince Yi Un.*

Middle Right: *Princess Yi Pang-ja (Masako) wife of Yi Un (Yongch'in-wang) mourns before her husband's memorial shrine in Naksonjae. Behind her stand Mrs. Yi Ku (Julia) and Princess Tok-hye.*

Bottom Left: *Princess Tok-hye, last living child of Ko-jong, resides in quiet seclusion in Naksonjae.*

Bottom Right: *The memorial altar for Yi Un was in Naksonjae before the funeral day.*

Left: *Mourners wait at the entrance of Naksonjae after the death of the heir apparent to the former throne of Yi. Yi Un (Yongch'in-wang) received the posthumous name of Ui-min which is written on the funeral banner.*

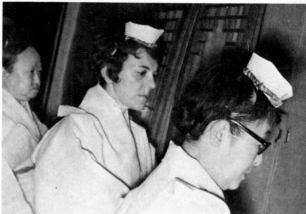

Top Left: *Mourners leave Naksonjae after offering their condolences to the Yi family of the late Yi Un (Yongch'in-wang).*
Top Right: *On the day of the funeral, May 9, 1970, the last crown prince of Yi is honored in a traditional ceremony of respect in front of Ch'angdok Palace.*
Bottom: *Music of sadness-blends with mournful cries as court musicians pay tribute to the passing of a dynasty.*

Top Left: *The funeral procession of Yi Un wends slowly out the gates of Naksonjae, led by Mr. Yi Ku (Yi Un's son), Princess Yi Pang-ja and Julia Lee.*

Top Right: *Princess Yi Pang-ja (Masako) pauses in solemn sorrow before a door opening to the gardens of Naksonjae. Dressed in mourning cloth she honors her husband's death.*

Bottom: *Under the eaves and* chapsang *the bier with the body of Yi Un makes its sad journey. Military guards stand in honor. This same bier was also used in the funeral ceremony for Queen Yun.*

Left Page: *The evening mist settles behind the back walls of Naksonjae. The last prince of Yi has died and mourners now dressed in sackcloth pause in grief outside the room where the body lies.*

Top: *The photograph of Yi Un (Yongch'in-wang) heads the funeral procession. The ROK honor guards enter Naksonjae to carry out the casket.*

Bottom: *The heavy casket made of pine wood is carried from Naksonjae. Yi Un spent his last six years in the hospital after coming to Korea in 1963; however, he wished to die at home. He arrived at Naksonjae three hours before his death on May 1, 1970.*

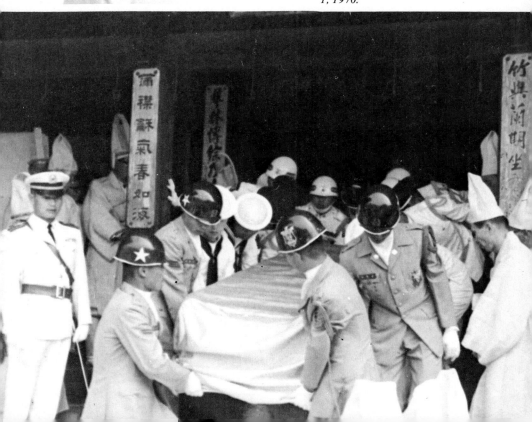

Top: *Normally 190 men are needed to carry the royal bier, but today it has been motorized. Brightly colored curtains seen through gauze and tassels produce an effect of Oriental splendor. Images of pheasant heads decorate corners while lotus blossoms form the base design. (Notice the strange unexplained reversal of the swastika symbols on the bier. In Asian Buddhism the arms normally turn to the left. The President of Dongguk University, Dr. Hwang Su-young indicated that this reversal of the Buddhist symbol was occasionally seen on Koryo bells.)*

Bottom: *Carrying the photograph, spirit tablet and box of personal effects to the tomb site are three of the sons of Uich'in-wang, nephews of the deceased.*

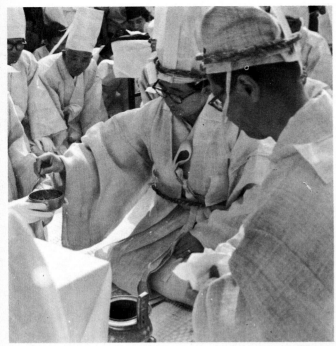

Left: *Mr. Yi Ku offers wine to the spirit of his father Yi Un (Yongch'in-wang) at his tomb site near Kumgok. The bamboo staff on the ground indicates the death of a father.*
Bottom: *The red banner of silk on which the name Uimin (posthumous name of Yi Un) has been written in gold letters is laid across the coffin. This banner was carried to the tomb site at the head of the procession. Usually in the final ritual, the* paebaek *representing the opposite forces of* um *and* yang *are laid over the coffin with the silk banner.*

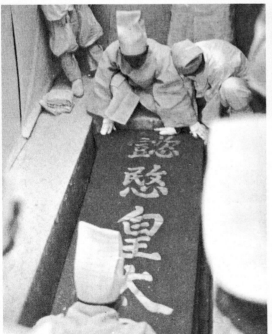

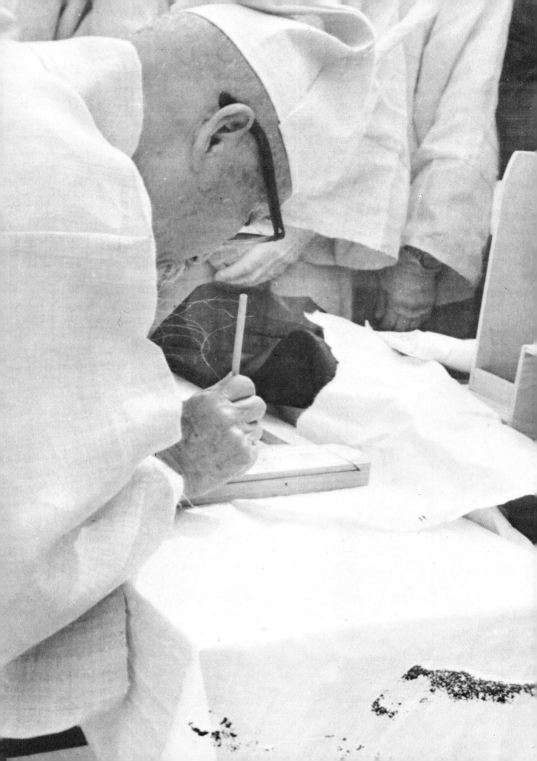

Left: *At the tomb site on the royal* wip'ae *(spirit tablet) is written the posthumous name of Ui-min. Mr. Yi Kun-han carefully writes the traditional Chinese characters. This tablet will remain for three years at the shrine for mourning in Naksonjae.*

Above: *The wail of* aigo *is heard as people gather on the hillsides near Kumgok to mourn the passing of a prince of Yi and the close of a dynasty.*

Sunwon-jon

Nungh

Area now called
Shinsonwon-jon

Gate to Sonwon-jon

SECRET GARDEN (Piwon)

To Ch'angdok Palace

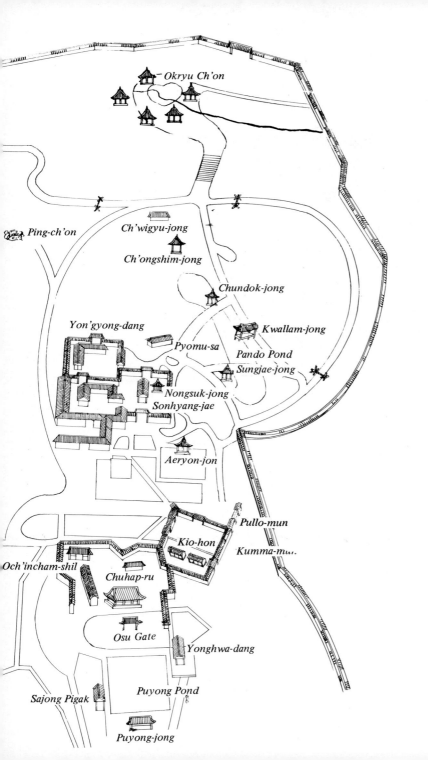

Okryu Ch'on

Ping-ch'on

Ch'wigyu-jong

Ch'ongshim-jong

Chundok-jong

Yon'gyong-dang

Kwallam-jong

Pyomu-sa

Pando Pond

Sungjae-jong

Nongsuk-jong

Sonhyang-jae

Aeryon-jon

Pullo-mun

Kio-hon

Kumma-mun

Och'incham-shil

Chuhap-ru

Osu Gate

Yonghwa-dang

Sajong Pigak

Puyong Pond

Puyong-jong

Puyong-jong and Puyong-ji

Upon entering the Secret Garden one first approaches a large lotus pond with a small island in the middle. This pond and the small pavilion to the left which extends over the water is called Puyong-ji and Puyong-jong. It is stated that this pond was fed by four springs but today these springs can not be found. A small tablet on the west side constructed by Suk-jong (19th king) tells of the discovery of these four springs. The twenty-sided pavillion is of unusual construction and was built in 1792 by Chong-jo (22nd king).

As a boy, King Chong-jo survived a tragic era of party conflict and mounted the throne upon the death of his grandfather Yong-jo (21st king). Chong-jo's own father had been falsely accused of insurrection and condemned to die by Yong-jo in 1762. Chong-jo was only a boy of ten at the time. King Chong-jo might be considered the last of the great scholar kings and his reign, which closed the eighteenth century, marks an era referred to as the second cultural revival of the Yi Dynasty. Known for his clever puns and riddles, this king spoke the dialects of the different prefectures and often capitalized on their colloquialisms for the sake of a joke.

The stimulus of Western thought sparked a break from the past. Priests arrived, and soon books describing Western inventions and achievements were written in Korean, as were books on law and music. A sizable Christian church developed within the country without missionary efforts, even though Christianity was strictly forbidden.

The interesting story of *hwa-do-hwa* and the renowned Ch'oe Che-gong is retold to illustrate the scholarly endeavors of King Chong-jo. Ch'oe was unusually brilliant and, because he was close to the king, often argued with him in a friendly manner about intricacies in the realm of higher academics. Scholar Ch'oe usually won the rounds. When King Chong-jo's emissaries went to China to visit, they learned of a flower that bloomed twice called *hwa-do-hwa* (flower-seed-flower). Actually this was the cotton plant, which was relatively unknown to Korea. Upon returning, Chong-jo decided *hwa-do-hwa* would make an excellent subject for the government exams, but he was reluctant to suggest it while scholar Ch'oe was still alive. The king knew that the aged scholar's great knowledge would discover the secret, thus humbling the king. Chong-jo bided his time and eventually Ch'oe Che-gong was gathered to his ancestors. The next year Chong-jo used *hwa-do-hwa* as the subject for the examination.

A week before the exam a poor country scholar came to Seoul and submitted his application. Since he could not afford the cost of a room at an inn, he slept beside the tomb of scholar Ch'oe. The night before the exam, the young man dreamed that this famous scholar appeared to him and told him not to worry and gave him the answer. The next day the country scholar went with many others to Yonghwa-dang, a pavilion east of the lotus pond where the exams were to take place. All failed the subject of *hwa-do-hwa* except the humble scholar from the south. King Chong-jo was surprised, and calling this young man to him, asked how he could possibly know the answer. The scholar then told of his dream the night before at the tomb site of Ch'oe Che-gong. King Chong-jo sighed. He realized that the venerable scholar had outwitted him again.

Chuhap-ru and Osu-mun

Opposite the lotus pond, the gate Osu-mun (Fish Water Gate) stands before the Chuhap Pavilion. The architectural design of this gate is impressive since the heavy roof is supported only by two small pillars. This gate and Chuhap-ru were built during the time of the American Revolutionary War. The aging Yong-jo (21st king) was then eighty-two and had ruled for fifty-two years, longer than any other Yi Dynasty king. The lower floor was used as a royal library while the top floor, overlooking the spacious gardens provided a place for entertainment and feasts.

King Yong-jo wished to live as frugally as possible. The story is told that one day while traveling incognito through the capital he captured a whiff of a most delicious dish being prepared by the wife of a poor merchant. After inquiring what it was, he asked his queen to make some for him. The queen directed the cooks to prepare it for her husband. Shortly afterward the court ladies brought many fancy dishes of food, but the king became angry. He had only wanted his queen to cook millet so that he could enjoy a simple meal of *chobap*. The queen bemoaned the fact that pleasing him was impossible.

When Queen So died at sixty-four, King Yong-jo married a twelve-year-old girl who became his new queen. King Yong-jo late in life once asked a

Yon'gyong-dang

Built in 1828 in the style of a typical home of a commoner's family during the reign of Sun-jo (23rd king), Yon'gyong-dang is the maximum size under Yi Dynasty laws, which forbade anyone other than royalty to have a house of more than 100 *kan* (one *kan* is about thirty-six square feet). Volcanic rocks displayed before the gate of this home were brought from the Diamond Mountains. Between the first and second entrances, a bell-shaped rock is seen which at one time was the container for a royal placenta. One stone cistern at the entrance of Yon'gyong-dang illustrates the humor of the Koreans. Small stone turtles carved in relief are seen crawling in and out of the cistern.

In 1884, when the reformist leaders attempted a coup d'etat, they fled to Yon'gyong-dang and held King Ko-jong prisoner. Before the construction of this elaborate home, the eighteen-year-old son of the king presented Sun-jo with his one and only grandson. The hereditary line seemed secure; yet within three years Sun-jo's son Ik-jong had died at twenty-one. When

King Sun-jo died four years later this young grandson of seven was suddenly thrust upon the throne as Hon-jong (24th king). The powerful dowager Queen Kim from Andong, wife of King Sun-jo, became regent for the boy. Even though the crown prince Ik-jong never ruled, he was given a king's burial at Tonggu-nung and after the mourning period his tablet was placed at the Chong-jon in Chongmyo, where the •more contributing kings of the Yi Dynasty are enshrined.

Ik-jong's wife lived to be eighty-one, and was responsible for helping place King Ko-jong on the throne in 1864. King Hon-jong had no sons by his two queens and his many concubines, but he is known for his congenial personality. If he had lived, he probably would have been a conscientious ruler. His passion for the palace women proved to be his undoing and he died of a venereal disease at the age of twenty-two.

Behind Yon'gyong-dang is the quiet and peaceful glen with a spring called Ping-ch'on (氷川). This area is considered to be the center of the Secret Gardens. Like Okryu-ch'on the water is safe to drink. Visitors should try some as the quality and flavor is excellent.

Yon'gyong-dang

*The beauty of each season portrays
a richness of nature in the Secret Gardens
of Ch'angdok Palace. Sunlight filters as
silver threads veiling the memory of the
past when rulers, courtiers and
courtesans wandered among the myriad
pleasure pavilions and along the streams
and ponds. The whisper of spring
alludes to voices from days gone by
while along the garden lanes and palace
walls the yesterdays are more fresh than
todays.*

Yonghwa-dang

The Flower-Reflecting Pavilion, which is located east of the first lotus pond upon entering the Secret Garden, was constructed by the "fortress-building" monarch Suk-jong (19th king) in 1692. Used for conducting public examinations to determine qualified aspirants for jobs as government officials, Yonghwa-dang was also used as a quiet place for meditation. Korea had succeeded in closing her doors to the outside world and was now at peace with her neighbors. Yet King Suk-jong's reign was far from tranquil, due to party strife and internal court bickering caused by the king's favorite, Chang Hui-bin. At Yonghwa-dang, King Suk-jong occasionally wrote poetry.

Pando-ji and Kwallam-jong

Considered by many to be the most picturesque pond within the Secret Garden is Pando-ji (Peninsula Pond). A small fan-shaped tea house constructed over the water lilies is reflected against the blue hues of the sky and restful shades of green from the surrounding foliage. First envisioned by In-jo (16th king) in 1646 as a quiet fishing hideaway, it undoubtedly symbolized the release from pressures of the Manchu invasion and the hope for prosperity. King In-jo's sons had been freed from Manchurian captivity the year before, and three years later the second son became Hyo-jong (17th king).

It is told that an extremely beautiful daughter of a Japanese nobleman who was quite talented in martial skills wanted to marry a husband from abroad. So, cutting her hair, she disguised herself as a Buddhist nun and came to Korea. She posted herself in front of Ch'angdok Palace. Soon she noticed that an unusually handsome boy in his teens often entered the palace and discovered that he was Prince Pong-im, the second son of the king. After devious efforts on her part, a mutual affection developed. The girl was invited into the palace, placed in a room and instructed to stay there for one year until her hair grew out. She read and studied during this time. When one year had almost passed, a guard came to Pong-im with the disconcerting news that his favorite white horse had been stolen and the young Japanese girl was missing from her room. Prince Pong-im found a note. In the letter the girl thanked the prince for all that he had done, but she had decided that she could not marry him, since he could never be a great person. The young prince was troubled, and pondered about this blunt allegation.

Several years later in 1637 Korea met defeat when the Manchu armies forced the king's surrender at Namhansan-song (South Fortress). Prince

Pong-im and his brother were carried away as captives. Eight years later, when the sons had been given their freedom, the Manchurian emperor announced that his queen wished to see Prince Pong-im before he left. The young man was guided through the palace and brought to the door of the women's quarters. He was greeted by filmy silhouettes of the shapely bodies of young courtesaus silently drifting behind the curtains. When he saw that many were partially nude he immediately reasoned that the emperor was deliberately tricking him into committing an unpardonable sin. As he turned to flee a stunning woman rose gracefully from a couch to greet him. Prince Pong-im stammered an apology, saying that he had been instructed to meet the queen. Unexpectedly, in the Korean language, this vivacious queen asked, "Don't you know me?" Prince Pong-im their realized that the queen was the same girl who many years before had fled from his palace. "Why did you leave?" the prince asked. The woman replied that she had observed he always bolted doors in rooms where he stayed, and she reasoned that because of his inner fear he would never become a great man. She had later met the Manchurian king's son hunting in the mountains and married him.

She had recognized the prince when he first arrived as a prisoner, and, behind the scenes, had been responsible for his release. Prince Pong-im (King Hyo-jong) later became one of the more significant kings of the dynasty.

IV. Ch'anggyong Palace

Ch'anggyong Palace called Bright Rejoicing, once served as a detached palace during the Yi Dynasty. Ch'anggyong Palace was reconstructed in 1484 during the reign of Song-jong (9th Yi king). Of all the palaces, only this one contains an example of a throne hall of the early Yi period.

The reign of Song-jong closed a period of strong leadership by the Korean kings. His nonconformist son, Yonsan-gun, inherited the throne, and after his overthrow the Yi kings lost their supremacy and did not regain it for several hundred years. Yet this new era is referred to by Confucian scholars as a Golden Age, since the arts flourished. King Song-jong was the grandson of Se-jo (7th king), who took away the throne from his nephew Tan-jong. King Se-jo died in 1468 and Song-jong came to the throne after the death of Ye-jong (8th king), who ruled less than a year.

History sometimes has a strange way of repeating itself. In 1096 the uncle of the fourteenth king of Koryo drove his nephew from the throne and became King Suk-jong. The most important event during the reign of Suk-jong (15th Koryo king) was his effort to establish a second capital at Seoul, then called Hanyang. The renowned Priest To-son who had prophesied the founding of the Koryo Dynasty had also declared that the capital must be moved from Songdo after one hundred and sixty years. Historians are certain that a Koryo palace was constructed in the southern area of the Ch'anggyong Palace, giving this site the oldest history of any of Seoul's palaces.

Priest To-son had also foretold the founding of the Yi Dynasty with its capital in Seoul. Fearful that moving the capital from Songdo (Kaesong) to Seoul might encroach upon the prophetic right of the future Yi Dynasty, King Ye-jong (son of Koryo King Suk-jong) decided on the alternate site of Pyongyang (now the north Korean capital).

Ye-jong (16th Koryo king) became an enthusiastic botanist, gathering rare plants from all over Korea and sending them to China in exchange for

CH'ANGGYONG PALACE

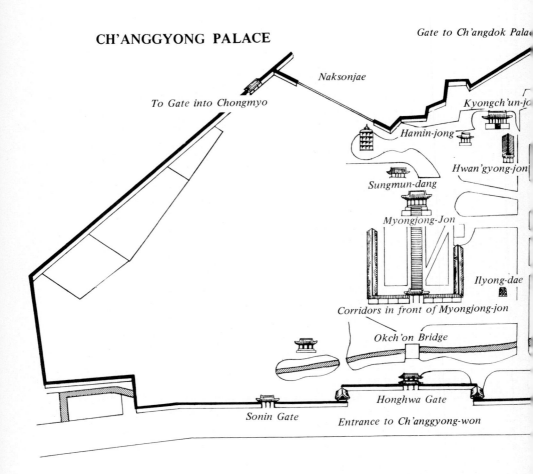

Gate to Ch'angdok Palace

Naksonjae

To Gate into Chongmyo

Kyongch'un-jo

Hamin-jong

Hwan'gyong-jon

Sungmun-dang

Myongjong-Jon

Ilyong-dae

Corridors in front of Myongjong-jon

Okch'on Bridge

Honghwa Gate

Sonin Gate

Entrance to Ch'anggyong-won

Parking Area in SNU Hospital

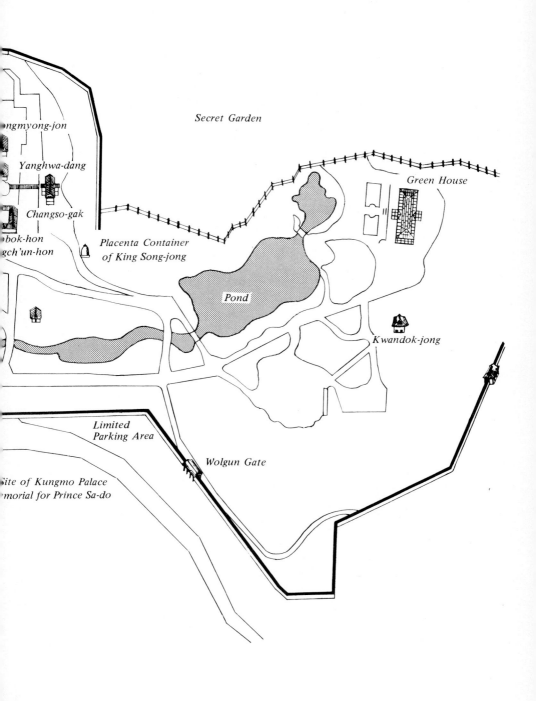

Secret Garden

ngmyong-jon

Yanghwa-dang

Green House

Changso-gak

Placenta Container
of King Song-jong

bok-hon
gch'un-hon

Pond

Kwandok-jong

Limited
Parking Area

Wolgun Gate

Site of Kungmo Palace
morial for Prince Sa-do

many varieties not found here. Coincidentally, in 1907 when Sun-jong (27th Yi king) moved to Ch angdok Palace, botanical and zoological gardens were built. It might be said that Koryo King Ye-jong's dream of a botanical garden reached fulfillment in Ch'anggyong, where a palace had been built originally in 1104 by his father, King Suk-jong (15th Koryo king).

This earlier palace was first occupied by T'ae-jo (1st Yi king) while Kyongbok was being constructed and also served as T'ae-jong's retirement palace in 1419, but after this period the palace fell into disrepair. During the Hideyoshi invasion of 1592, most of the palace buildings were burned. Myongjong-jon, the main audience hall, which faces east rather than south, with its surrounding corridors is believed to have survived this fire. Most of the other buildings were rebuilt during the reign of Sun-jo (23rd king) in 1833.

In 1907 the title of Ch'anggyong Palace was changed from *kung* (palace) to *won* (garden) by the Japanese. When the Japanese authorities made this palace a botanical garden and zoo, the intent was to subtly weaken the influence of the royalty and deliberately humble the king by taking his land and turning it into a domain for animals and birds.

However, during the Japanese occupation period the authorities did develop this wooded palace area into one of the finest zoos and botanicial gardens in Asia. Since the Korean War it was revived and further developed. Up until several years ago Ch'anggyong Palace was one of the most popular places to visit with a family during pleasant weather, especially in the spring and fall. Cherry trees, which are indigenous to Korea, were planted throughout the grounds. Usually during the cherry blossom festival the palace grounds were opened in the evening with lights and attracted blossom viewers from all over Korea.

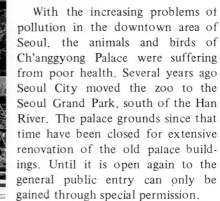

With the increasing problems of pollution in the downtown area of Seoul, the animals and birds of Ch'anggyong Palace were suffering from poor health. Several years ago Seoul City moved the zoo to the Seoul Grand Park, south of the Han River. The palace grounds since that time have been closed for extensive renovation of the old palace buildings. Until it is open again to the general public entry can only be gained through special permission.

Honghwa Gate

There are two entrances generally used for Ch'anggyong Palace. The back gate, which is often closed, is located near the entrance gate to the Secret Garden and between Naeui-won and Naksonjae. The main gate of Ch'anggyong Palace called Honghwa-mun or Gate of Vast Transformation is recommended though it is difficult on crowded days to find a parking place on the street in front. (A parking lot has been developed near SNU Hospital.) This impressive double-roofed wooden gate faces east rather than south. Traditionally Koryo palaces faced east, whereas the Chinese and Yi Dynasty palaces would face south. As this site was used as a palace during the Koryo era this fact might explain why the main gate as well as the entire palace complex including the main audience hall faces east. Honghwa Gate is listed as cultural treasure #384. Directly behind Honghwa-mun is the royal stream crossed by a bridge called Stream of Jewels. A bridge and stream located immediately inside the main gate of any palace or tomb site is true to correct architectural design. Ch'anggyong Palace though facing east and never again occupied by Korean kings since the time of T'ae-jo (1st king) is still no exception to a typical palace arrangement.

Okch'on Bridge

After passing through the main entrance of the impressive Honghwa Gate, the central route leads over a stone bridge with twin arch supports. This type of bridge is an integral part of palace architecture. Okch'on is the oldest palace entrance bridge in Seoul and has been designated a cultural treasure.

The bridge was built during Song-jong's reign at the time of the palace's original construction. On the bridge, a *haet'ae* (fire-eating monster) sits at each corner railing, while water lily buds are depicted on the four upright railing posts spanning the stream. It is interesting to note that between every two posts is one unbroken stone carved to represent a joining of several pieces. Under the bridge between the two arches is the face of a *tokkeibi* in relief.

Myongjong-jon

This palace throne hall fortunately escaped destruction during the 1592 Hideyoshi conquest and now remains as the oldest audience chamber of any Yi Dynasty palace. This single-roof structure was built in 1483 during the reign of Song-jong (9th king). In front of this building a double-level walkway leads westward toward two series of steps with carved stone railings depicting the *haet'ae*, imaginary fire-eating monster who supposedly protects the building from fire. On either side of the walkway are twelve stone markers for the officials ranked closest to the king. As one faces the audience hall, the civilian officials are on the right while the military officials are on the left. Inside the building, the phoenix, symbol of immortality, can be seen in the center of the ceiling, and behind the throne is a screen similar to the one more fully described in the Ch'angdok Palace. To the rear of this building can be seen the remnants of a second-level roof which had been a continuation of a passageway exiting to annex buildings on either side. In-jong (12th king), who ruled only one year and died under mysterious circumstances, was enthroned in this hall in 1544. His half brother Myong-jong became king after his death.

Myongjong Gate:

The main gate to the audience hall of Myongjong-jon is in a straight line between the audience hall and Honghwa Gate in an east-west direction. The gate faces east and is believed to be an older structure than Myongjong-jon. At one time corridors completely surrounded this courtyard and now part of them remain and are used for storage. The route from Okch'on Bridge through Myongjong Gate to the audience hall is considered the oldest original palace entrance for the city of Seoul.

Hamin-jong

This pavilion was originally built in 1633 by In-jo (16th king). The present structure dates to 1833 and was used as a resting area for royalty.

Ilyong-dae

Located north of the corridors of Myongjong-mun this pedestal for a sun dial was once located near Seoul's Little West Gate and was moved here in 1975.

second wife and queen to Suk-jong (19th king). Gentle and mild in spirit, she has been recorded in history as one of the great if not the greatest Yi Dynasty queens. After years of marriage to Suk-jong without producing children, she suggested that her husband take another wife. The king became infatuated with Chang, a court lady. Though extremely beautiful, Chang was jealous and cruel and sent thousands to their deaths. She succeeded in having Queen Min banished from the palace. Suk-jong, blind in his love for Chang Hui-bin, refused to discuss his irrational actions with any of his advisors.

The king, disguised as a *yangban* (rich gentry), occasionally traveled about the Korean countryside to see how his people were faring. Several years after his marriage to Chang, he came to a small village in a remote southern region and saw a group of children dancing in a circle and singing a rhyming song, *"changdari, minari; changdari, minari."* *Changdari* (turnip stalk) will only grow in one season. Certain turnips are saved over the winter and planted in spring only for the seed. The *changdari* is the stalk bearing the seeds for the fall turnips.

Minari (watercress) can grow in every season, even in water under ice, so is good for all seasons. The initial sound of the word for turnip stalk (*chang*) was used in reference to the unpredictable and changing concubine while the initial sound of the word for watercress (*min*) was used in reference to the true and faithful Queen Min.

The disguised king asked nearby farmers what the song meant. The farmers were aghast and asked, "Where are you from? You must not be Korean, since all Korea knows this song." The king was shocked and, lying, said that he had just arrived from China and was a stranger to these parts. The farmers related the tragedy that had befallen good Queen Min, a woman for all seasons, and the foolishness of the king in taking Chang Hui-bin for a wife.

Unable to stand this treasonous talk, the bodyguard started to attack the farmers, but was held back by Suk-jong, who said he really didn't see anything wrong with the king's actions. The farmers exclaimed in disgust, "Don't you have a stomach?" King Suk-jong returned to the palace pondering this affair. Finally Chang's deceit became evident to him and he reinstated Min as queen.

Chang Hui-bin then resorted to sorcery to have Queen Min killed. The beautiful and patient Queen Min was afflicted with boils which became so serious that she moved to Kyongch'un-jon and died there in September 1701. Despite her tragic life which ended so ignominiously, Queen Min was buried beside her husband at the West Five Tombs.

Yanghwa-dang

Yanghwa-dang was reconstructed several times after 1484 when it was first built. Its last construction was 1624. After the Manchu invasion, In-jo (16th king) lived here while palace reconstruction was being accomplished.

T'ongmyong-jon

Constructed in 1833 during the reign of Sun-jo (23rd king), this building was used to celebrate the royal *hwan'gap.* (one's sixtieth birthday). The *hwan'gap* or five zodiac cycles has special meaning for Koreans who have attained a full life and have been abundantly blessed. Like Taejo-jon in Ch'ang-dok Palace the central roof ridge is missing. The plaque was written by King Sun-jo. To the west is a picturesque rectangular stone pond with a bridge, stone railings and stone *haet'ae* on a pedestal. The unique feature is that the *haet'ae* has a baby curled beside the mother. The well nearby has a stone channel leading into the pond.

Yongch'un-hon and Chipbok-hon

During the reign of Sun-jo (23rd king), both of these living areas were destroyed by fire and were rebuilt three years later in 1833. Chang-jo (Prince Sa-do) was born in Chipbok-hon when Yong-jo (21st king) was ruler. At the age of twenty-seven the young prince was falsely accused of insurrection against King Yong-jo and condemned to die by being placed in a large rice box in front of Sonin Gate. Prince Sa-do's second son, who later became Chong-jo (22nd king), was only ten at the time of his father's murder. He continued to live in Yongch'un-hon even after he became king.

His grandfather, King Yong-jo, tried to erase from the boy's mind any loyalty toward his father. This he evidently failed to do. The story is told that King Yong-jo instructed the boy's tutor to neglect the teaching of

The Ch'anggyong Palace is a popular park area for both young and old especially during the cherry blossom season.

yo-ap'yon (the code of filial piety), but Chong-jo read and studied extensively about it anyway. The king became suspicious and decided to check the books the young prince was reading. Hong Kug-yong, the tutor, heard of this and went secretly to the boy's room where he cut away all the pages dealing with *yo-ap'yon*. When the young boy presented his books to his grandfather, Yong-jo was impressed that these pages were cut out. The tutor kept his positon and the boy was saved from a severe reprimand. Hong, who incidentally was the most talented *paduk* player in Korea at this time,

later became powerful and wealthy. He was appointed as a minister, but misused his authority.

After Chong-jo became king, an elaborate shrine called Kungmo-gung (Respect and Remember Palace) was erected on the grounds where Seoul National University Hospital stands. The Wolgun Gate, north of the Honghwa Gate, was built to be used exclusively by Chong-jo as he went frequently to his father's shrine to pay his respects.

Changso-gak

This Western style building portrays Japanese architecture with the Korean plum crest on the ridge. Built in 1911 as a museum it later became the royal library. Most of the rare library books have been moved to the Academy for Korean Studies, south of Seoul.

Sonin Gate

This small gate, reconstructed in 1857, is located south of Honghwa Gate on the eastern wall. It is famous for two events that took place during the Yi Dynasty. The first event marked the close of a tragic era of Korean history when the notorious Yonsan-gun (10th king) was overthrown and a half brother became Chung-jong (11th king) in 1506. The reign of terror created by the unworthy ruler Yonsan-gun had left the country reeling with horror and shock. When this king was banished, he departed into obscurity through this gate.

The second event, as has already been mentioned, is the death of Prince Sa-do, crown prince and son of Yong-jo (21st king), who was condemned to die behind this gate in 1762. The reason for this tragic murder is difficult to explain, but can possibly be credited to a senile father encumbered with poor judgment. Because Queen So had no children by Yong-jo, the son of the concubine Yi Chong-bin was declared crown prince. But this son, Chin-jong, died at the age of nine. After his death, party feuds between the Noron and Soron grew worse. King Yong-jo favored the Noron, though the Soron were probably more powerful. Prince Sa-do, a member of neither party, disagreed with his father who thought that all Soron members should be killed. The Noron party then began to plan the killing of Prince Sa-do, since his leniency toward the Soron party further endangered their own party.

Entire villages were massacred and clues were left deliberately to implicate Prince Sa-do. Doctors were bribed to give certain medicines to Prince Sa-do to weaken him physically. Princess Hwa-hwan, one of Prince Sa-do's own sisters, actively helped to plot his death, and it has been said she originated the idea of using a rice box to execute Prince Sa-do. Hwa-hwan's husband had been expelled from the palace because of a fight he had with Sa-do. Mun So-ui, another concubine of King Yong-jo, also hated Prince Sa-do and his mother. The reason for this may have been because she had no children. Needless to say, Prince Sa-do had many enemies. Queen Kim (third queen of Suk-jong) and Queen So (first queen of Yong-jo) seemed to be the only royal family members loyal to the prince, and when they both died in 1757 Prince Sa-do's ultimate fate was sealed. Even his wife's father, Hong Pong-han, tried to have him ostracized from court.

By planting weapon caches around the countryside, the Noron party finally convinced the king that Prince Sa-do was planning a revolt. The enraged king during Sa-do's trial commanded soldiers to put him in a rice box in the court behind Sonin gate. It has been claimed that a certain Ku,

the official boxkeeper, on his own initiative (more likely he was bribed by the Noron Party) burned grass next to the box to make it even hotter inside, although it was mid-July.

One loyal subject, a man called Han Kon, came faithfully each day to the box and cried for one hour. At this time, he would drop small grains of raw rice through a knothole for Sa-do to eat. He was eventually discovered and exiled to a distant island. After twenty-one days the box was opened and Prince Sa-do was found dead.

On the day that Prince Sa-do's son became king, he had boxkeeper Ku beheaded. He also killed all Norons and the house of Hong (father of his mother). His mother pleaded with him to spare one person to care for the family tomb, so he did not kill her father. The evil sister was exiled, and went to live with the tombkeeper who tended the grave of Ch'oe Suk-bin (mother of King Yong-jo).

Additional Points of Interest

Located behind the library (Changso-gak) is a stone turtle bearing a small tablet designating the resting place of the umbilical cord of Song-jong (9th king), founder of this palace. This placenta container was moved to this site in 1823. During the Japanese occupation all umbilical cord burials were moved to So-sam-nung, so it is likely this container is empty.

At birth there is an elaborate ceremony during which time the umbilical cord and afterbirth are placed in a small jar, which in turn is placed in a larger jar. The larger jar is then put in the stone container seen at this site, and a large stone cap placed over the huge bell-shaped bowl. The umbilical cord of a commoner is merely thrown onto the thatched roof and left to dry.

Until recent years the lake in Ch'anggyong Palace would be crowded with sightseers in brightly colored rowboats. Once this area was farmland within the palace grounds. This field was divided into eight sections, representing Korean provinces during Yi Dynasty times. The success or failure of the crops in each particular section of the field was an indication of the expected crop yield in the different regions of the kingdom.

On a knoll near the lake is Kwandok-jong which was built as an archery range by In-jo (16th king). The archers shot from the knoll to a target in the Secret Garden.

Chapter V

Toksu Palace

As the Toksu Palace is located in the heart of Seoul City it remains most popular for Korean visitors. Within the walls the last of the great kings of the Yi Dynasty died in 1919 after annexation by the Japanese. King Ko-jong abdicated in 1907 and Korea was annexed in 1910.

TOKSU PALACE

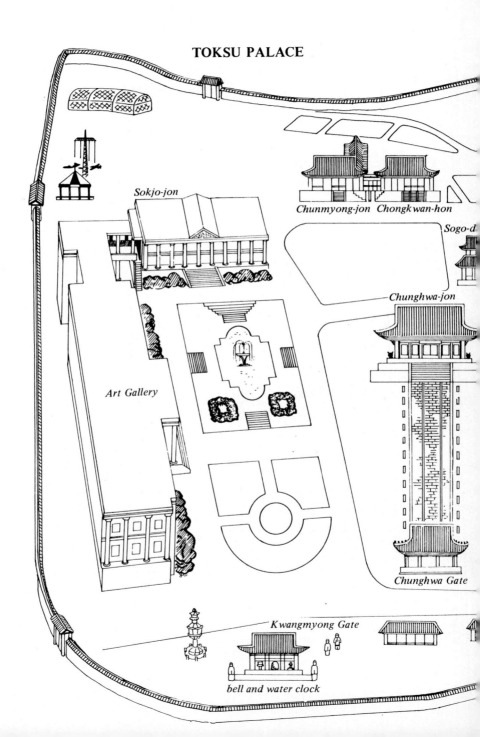

Sokjo-jon

Chunmyong-jon　Chongkwan-hon

Sogo-d

Chunghwa-jon

Art Gallery

Chunghwa Gate

Kwangmyong Gate

bell and water clock

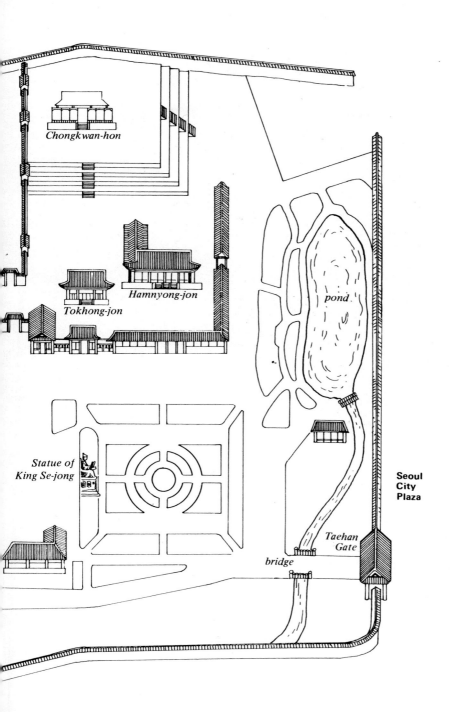

Chongkwan-hon

Hamnyong-jon

Tokhong-jon

pond

Statue of
King Se-jong

Seoul
City
Plaza

Taehan
Gate

bridge

V. Toksu Palace

These well-known gardens and palace buildings, located between the capitol building and South Gate, do not exhibit the traditional style of a Yi Dynasty palace. Nevertheless, the old National Museum and Fine Arts Building and the few remaining historic palace structures will provide an interesting afternoon for any visitor. It was here that the five hundred years of Yi Dynasty rule drew to a painful and tragic end as Japanese domination finally resulted in annexation.

Following the murder of his queen, Ko-jong (26th king) fled to the Russian Legation in February 1896. During his thirteen-month residence in the legation Lady Om conceived and after a normal pregnancy gave birth to Yi Un (Yongch'in-wang) in 1897. A portion of the Russian Legation can still be seen. King Ko-jong this same year moved to the Toksu Palace and made it the seat of government. After abdicating in 1907 he also used Toksu for his retirement.

Toksu Palace was originally a royal villa constructed to appease a grandson of Se-jo (7th Yi king) who was passed over and did not become a king. King Se-jo ruthlessly snatched the kingdom from King Tan-jong, his nephew, and eventually had him murdered in 1457. Se-jo's eldest son Tok-jong also died that same year. The title of crown prince might well have gone to Tok-jong's eldest son, Wolsan-taegun, but instead went to Ye-jong second son of Se-jo by Queen Yun. It has been suggested by authorities that to justify his action Se-jo claimed Wolsan-taegun was mentally deranged, and there is also a hint that Se-jo himself caused the insanity by administering herbs. Even though Ye-jong (8th king) had two sons before he died at the age of nineteen, the second son of Tok-jong (younger brother of Wolsan-taegun) was selected to become Song-jong (9th king) in 1469, either because Ye-jong's sons were too young or because of the dominating power of the regent Yun (Se-jo's queen).

Prince Wolsan was loved and respected by all, including his younger brother who became King Song-jong. He was an avid reader and patron of

Chunghwa-jon

The audience hall, originally a double-roofed building, was reconstructed with only one roof after the great fire of 1904. A raised two-level walkway goes from the gate to the hall. The king used the center, while high-ranking subjects walked on either side. Flagstones originally covered the entire court area. On either side a series of stone markers indicate the order of rank of civil and military officials. As the king faced the court, the military would be on his right and civil officials on his left. Additional *haet'ae* are seen at the steps, and as one peers into the hall itself, the *yongsang* (dragon seat) is seen in the center in front of a large painting. The dragon theme, symbol of royalty, is prevalent throughout the design of the throne chair. The dilapidated painting behind it is credited to the Japanese. The gold sun-like circles represent the west (sun) and the east (moon). When an official was granted an audience, he sent a representative up the stairs and into the hall while he remained standing by his identifying stone marker.

Occasionally, important messages were altered by dishonest couriers during this short walk to the king. The huge incense burners located on the corners of the platform were lit during a royal audience. The hazy smoke drifted skyward to join celestial beings as a reminder that the king was one with the gods and would certainly discover dishonesty. Therefore, only the truth must be reported to the king.

On the eaves of the roof can be seen *chapsang* (clay figurines) which are believed to help protect the building from fire. These clay figures are found only at temples, palace buildings, or gates which the king might use. The maximum number in Korea is nine, while in China the imperial rooftop figurines might total twelve.

Chunghwa Gate

In accordance with palace architecture, there is a stone bridge to cross after entering the palace grounds. Pass a small pavilion on the right, and enter the gate to Chunghwa-jon (main audience hall), which opens into the final approach to the main hall. There are three series of steps in front of the three doorways to this gate; the king used only the middle entrance. The royal dragon insignia is in the center flanked by four *haet'ae* (fire-eating monsters) on the step railings. This animal is believed to protect buildings from fire.

Sogo-dang

Sogo-dang (Old Royal Hall) is an impressive double-roof structure and the only two-story building remaining from the early days. King Son-jo lived here for sixteen years after returning from the Yalu River where Hideyoshi's armies had sent him fleeing. King Son-jo had no sons by his queens, and Prince Kwang-hae, son of concubine Kim, was given the title of crown prince. But just before the king's death, Queen Kim (In-mok) bore a son, causing jealousy to develop into hatred when the king tried to take the title from Kwang-hae and give it to the new son. The king died and the hapless youth was soon taken from his mother's arms. Under orders from Kwang-hae, the governor of Kanghwa Island put the boy in an *ondol* room which was heated until the youth suffocated. The king unmercifully continued persecuting Queen Kim, but he was finally overthrown and banished.

While King Ko-jong was living at the Russian Legation after the murder of Queen Min, he had Sogo-dang renovated and used it as his residence from 1897.

Sokjo-jon and Art Gallery

Sokjo-jon which was the National Museum, was designed in 1901 by Mr. H. W. Davidson, an English architect who used a Renaissance style. It was completed in 1909. The daughter of Mr. Davidson later married Dr. Horace G. Underwood, now of Yonsei University.

No special name was given to the structure as it has always been called "stone-made hall." Ko-jong used the building to entertain ranking foreign diplomats. Used as an art exhibition hall during the Japanese occupation, it became important after World War II as headquarters for the American-Soviet Commission for the Unification of Korea. At the outbreak of the Korean War, the UN Commission moved into the building.

From 1955 this building served as Korea's National Museum under the directorship of Dr. Kim Jae-won. In 1972 the National Museum moved to its present location in Kyongbok Palace under the directorship of Dr. Hwang Su-young; The public is indebted to the retired director, Dr. Kim Jae-won, who over the many years has developed the museum to the high standard that it maintains today.

In 1938 the Yi Household Museum opened its doors here under the auspices of the Office of Cultural Preservation. It is now an art gallery with a fine collection of paintings, calligraphy, sculptures and many outstanding Koryo porcelains.

142

Chukjo-dang

One of the two buildings not destroyed during the Hideyoshi invasion is Chukjo-dang. In-jo (16th king) was forced to flee to Kongju during a rebellion instigated by Yi Kwal, a disgruntled official. This rebellion was quickly put down and King In-jo was reinstated in a ceremony held in this hall. Thus the name Chukjo-dang (Ascension Hall) came into being.

Tokhong-jon and Hamnyong-jon

As one gazes over the famous peony gardens from the windows of the the *tabang,* one sees clearly the inner palace residence. On the right is a hall used for exhibitions. In the center and to the left are two buildings which were used exclusively by the king and his wives during his days of retirement. The larger building, the Hamnyong-jon, contained the royal bedroom; it is here that King Ko-jong died on January 21, 1919. Prince Yuk, son of

Ko-jong by Kwanghwa-dang (royal concubine), was born near here but died twenty months later. After Ko-jong's death the palace was closed and fell into disrepair. Toksu Palace was first opened to the public in 1933.

Toksu Palace Bell

In one corner of the palace grounds is a bronze Chinese-style bell which was cast in 1396 to honor Queen Kang, second wife of T'ae-jo (1st Yi King). This bell was originally located at Hungch'on-sa in Seoul. Its unusual feature consists of two belts encircling the mid-section, a characteristic not often found on Korean bells. Next to the bell is a water clock made in 1536 and is one of the oldest of its kind in the world. A turtle-shaped arrow floats on the water which indicates the correct time. This bell and clock are located in Kwangmyong-mun, a gate of Toksu Palace which was once located in front of Hamnyong-jon. It was moved here in 1938. Surrounding this pavilion-like gate are stone statues of civil officials, possibly brought from royal grave sites.

Above: *Statue of King Se-jong, 4th ruler of Yi Dynasty*
Left: *Sokjo-jon, fine art gallery*

Chongkwan-hon

Eastward from Sogo-dang is a wall which contains five differently styled gates. All of these gates lead into the compound where King Ko-jong died in 1919. Previously, each gate led into a separate enclosure bounded by a tiled wall. The buildings were destroyed in the fire of 1904 and were never replaced; later, the walls were demolished. One can only imagine the network of palace architecture that once dominated this area. In the northern part of this enclosure is a *tabang* (tea house) which was used by King Ko-jong as a place of entertainment.

Chunmyong-jon

Chunmyong-jon was used as a residence for King Ko-jong and was rebuilt in 1906. The portraits of the last two kings were enshrined here but have been removed. It was the residence of Yi Un (son of Ko-jong by Om Kwibi) and wife Yi Pang-ja (Masako) during their visit from Japan in 1922, but after their first son died as an infant in this home, it was left unoccupied.

Statue of King Se-jong

In 1968 a statue of Se-jong, fourth king of the Yi Dynasty, was erected. King Se-jong, the most famous of all Yi kings, began his rule in 1418 which was highlighted by scientific inventions and literary development.

He appointed a group of scholars to develop a Korean alphabet so that the lower classes might be provided with books they could read in their own language. Prior to this all literature was in Chinese. King Se-jong perfected and financed moveable metal type, the first to be used in the world. This took place fifty years before Gutenberg's invention in Germany. Though appreciated by the masses, the new alphabet offended many of the ranking scholars of that day, who felt the classics were being "dragged in the dust" by becoming available to the people. Chinese literature was now accessible and began to penetrate for the first time into Korean culture, stimulating and enriching local literature, which evolved slowly. During the periods of weak kings and strong court officials, *han'gul* was relegated to less importance and finally not used. As a result of the efforts of the first Christian missionaries to Korea, *han'gul* was brought out of disuse to become the common written language. King Se-jong officially gave *han'gul* to the people in 1446. Now the ninth day of October has become Han'gul Day, a national holiday.

Chapter VI

Chongmyo (Royal Ancestral Shrine)

Chong-jon
Yongnyong-jon
Entry of Spirit Tablet of Yun, Last Queen of Korea
Main Gate of Chongmyo Shrine

VI. Chongmyo (Royal Ancestral Shrine)

In a secluded garden near the heart of Seoul lies Chongmyo, which houses the ancestral tablets of Yi Dynasty kings and queens. It is here that one can visualize the pomp and ceremony of the Confucian memorial services held five times a year from the reign of dynasty founder Yi T'ae-jo (1392). Chongmyo was first opened to the public in 1960. The shrine is composed of two major buildings, Chong-jon and Yongnyong-jon. Entering the main gate, the first buildings one sees on the right (1) were used until 1945 as a place for planning ceremonies and are now the park offices.

In the compound of buildings (2) farther on, various ritualistic articles are displayed. At the right of the center building is a fire cavity where the *ondol* floor was heated while the king changed into his ceremonial attire. A small palanquin can be seen which was used to carry the ancestral tablet to this resting place at Chongmyo. Many gold or jade *tojang* can be viewed. On these royal seals are the names of the Yi kings. They were used to seal government papers, thus making the documents official. Some musical instruments can also be seen at this museum.

The walkway (3) leading from the rear exit of the exhibition hall toward the kitchen is high in the center. The king would use the center lane and lesser nobles, either side. Before the walkway ends at the side gate, there is a small platform where the royal party would wait. It is on this platform (4) and others within the shrine enclosure that the king would wash his hands with water from the well (5) symbolizing purification. The platforms (6) in front of the kitchen may have been used for the preparation of food which was placed on the tables in front of each cubicle before the ceremony.

Notice the walkway in front of Chong-jon (7). It was constructed to make Chong-jon appear more spacious than it really is as one walks from the exhibition hall. Following the principle that parallel lines appear to join in the distance, this walkway was constructed nearer to the wall at the further end, thus giving the wall of Chong-jon an apparently greater length. The architectural skill of using natural contours for an excellent drainage system is noteworthy.

Confucian ceremonies are now conducted every spring in the courtyards of Chongmyo. Foreigners are cordially invited to attend. Yi Ku (below) is titular head of the Yi Dynasty Association (consisting of former royal family members and ancestors).

CHONGMYO

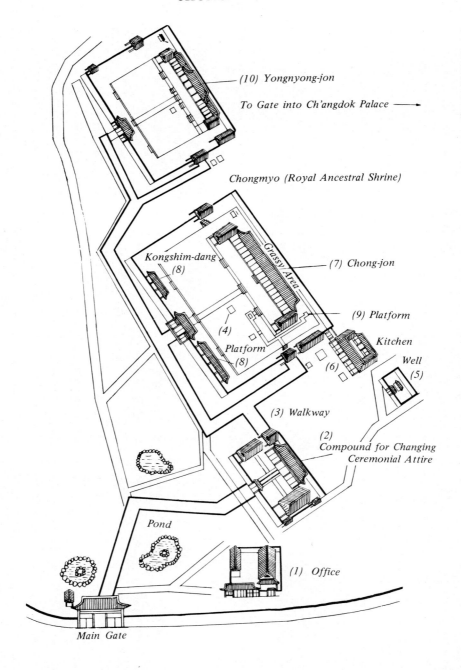

(10) Yongnyong-jon

To Gate into Ch'angdok Palace ⟶

Chongmyo (Royal Ancestral Shrine)

Kongshim-dang
(8)

(7) Chong-jon

Grassy Area

(9) Platform

(4)

Kitchen

Platform
(8)

Well
(5)

(6)

(3) Walkway

(2)
Compound for Changing
Ceremonial Attire

Pond

(1) Office

Main Gate

LOCATION CHART OF SPIRIT TABLETS AT CHONGMYO
(Royal Ancestral Shrine)

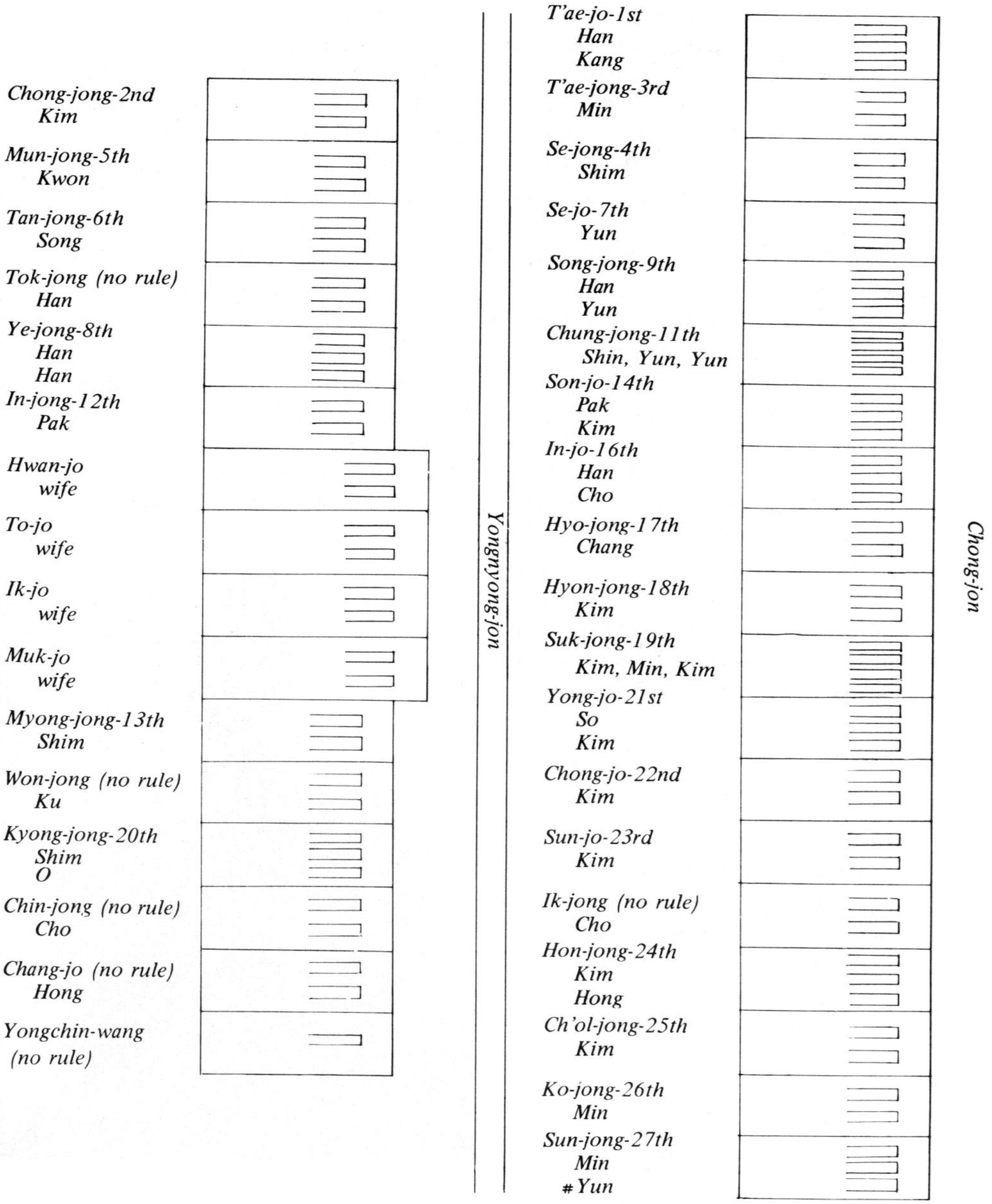

T'ae-jo-1st
Han
Kang

Chong-jong-2nd
Kim

T'ae-jong-3rd
Min

Mun-jong-5th
Kwon

Se-jong-4th
Shim

Tan-jong-6th
Song

Se-jo-7th
Yun

Tok-jong (no rule)
Han

Song-jong-9th
Han
Yun

Ye-jong-8th
Han
Han

Chung-jong-11th
Shin, Yun, Yun

In-jong-12th
Pak

Son-jo-14th
Pak
Kim

Hwan-jo
wife

In-jo-16th
Han
Cho

To-jo
wife

Hyo-jong-17th
Chang

Ik-jo
wife

Hyon-jong-18th
Kim

Muk-jo
wife

Suk-jong-19th
Kim, Min, Kim

Myong-jong-13th
Shim

Yong-jo-21st
So
Kim

Won-jong (no rule)
Ku

Chong-jo-22nd
Kim

Kyong-jong-20th
Shim
O

Sun-jo-23rd
Kim

Chin-jong (no rule)
Cho

Ik-jong (no rule)
Cho

Chang-jo (no rule)
Hong

Hon-jong-24th
Kim
Hong

Yongchin-wang
(no rule)

Ch'ol-jong-25th
Kim

Ko-jong-26th
Min

Sun-jong-27th
Min
#Yun

Yongnyong-jon

Chong-jon

#*October 1968 (last queen enshrined)*

Queen Yun, second wife of King Sun-jong and last queen of Korea

Entry of Spirit Tablet of Yun, Last Queen of Korea

On October 24, 1968, the tablet of Queen Yun, second wife of Sun-jong (27th king) and last queen of the Yi Dynasty, was officially enshrined in Chongmyo. To prevent an undue drain on finances, pomp and ceremony were held to a minimum. Queen Yun's tablet is now located in the very last cubicle on the right. For the ceremony the doors were opened for the first time since 1945. When Queen Yun was buried at Kumgok in February 1966, her ceremonial tablet was taken to her former home at Naksonjae. The three remaining *sanggung* (court ladies) prepared food twice daily for the spirit of the queen. At the close of the second year mourning period the tablet was moved to Chongmyo and its final resting place.

Mr. Yi Ku standing before the altar of departed queen.

As a murky drizzle fell in the cool autumn air, a box of the queen's personal effects wrapped with a bright red cloth was slowly carried by two men through the main gate of Chongmyo. Following closely, a small palanquin containing the spirit tablet of Queen Yun was carried by other assistants. The subdued colors of red and yellow leaves in the wooded area surrounding the courtyard blended with the glistening wet gray of stone, creating a melancholy atmosphere of serenity as the last of Yi royalty was officially placed in the ancestral shrine. Led by Yi Ku (Kyu Lee), grandson of the late King Ko-jong, formal respect was paid to all kings and queens enshrined in both buildings. Food and three chalices of wine were offered to the spirit represented by each tablet. Starting at seven in the morning, the ritual concluded at two o'clock in the afternoon.

Top Left: *The three* sanggung *(court ladies) who faithfully served Queen Yun during life now stand before the altar of their departed queen. Pak, left: served Queen Yun from her teen-age years; Kim, center: came to the palace with the queen at the time of her marriage in 1906; Song, right: is not a true* sanggung *since her service began after the close of the dynasty.*

Middle Left: *Princess Yi Pang-ja (Masako), left: wife of Yi Un (Yongch'in-wang) and mother of Yi Ku; Princess Tok-hye center: last living child of King Ko-jong; Mrs. Julia Lee, right: wife of Mr. Yi Ku. Hidden behind Mrs. Yi is Ko-jong's last living official wife Sam-ch'uk-dang who died September 23, 1970.*

Bottom Left: *Queen Yun's favorite foods are simplified because of current expenses. These dishes were prepared for the ceremony which concluded the mourning period. This final ceremony was held on the night of February 10, 1968 at the queen's former residence in Naksonjae.*

Right: *Mr. Yi Ku offering his respect in this ceremony at Naksonjae. Mr. Yi Su-gil is assisting on the right. This altar remained in Naksonjae three years following the death of Queen Yun. The spirit tablet is seen in the center.*

Bottom: *The royal bier slowly proceeded past East Gate on its way to Kumgok where the queen was buried on the afternoon of February 13, 1966.*

Top: *The spirit tablet altar of King Sun-jong at the right end of Chong-jon within Chongmyo is viewed for the first time by the public since 1945. From left to right are the* wip'ae *(spirit tablet) of King Sun-jong, Queen Min and Queen Yun. The round holes in the tablets are for carrying them to safety in time of war.*

Bottom: *Sweet wine in brass cups is raised to Yi rulers whose spirits are honored. Upon the death of Queen Yun the ancestors of Yi were notified with respect.*

Right Page: *Through these open gates a dynasty came to an end when the spirit tablet of Queen Yun, last queen of Korea, entered the shrine of Chong-jon in Chongmyo. The location of her shrine cubicle is being pointed out to Mr. Yi Ku (standing on the left) by Mr. Rii (Yi) Keun Woong, former president of the Yi Dynasty Relatives Association.*

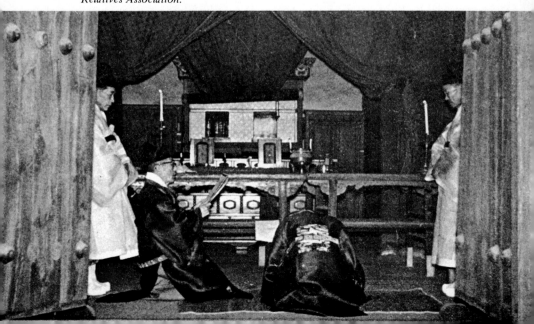

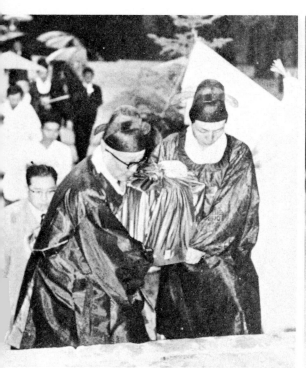

Left Page: *The palanquin carrying the tablet of Queen Yun and her personal belongings enter the courtyard of Chong-jon, the main shrine of Chongmyo.*

Top: *Within Chong-jon, the main shrine building in Chongmyo, are enshrined nineteen kings and their thirty queens. On the corridor porch of Chong-jon are nineteen tables with ceremonial utensils. There are two wine cups for each occupant. The table in the foreground is for Suk-jong (19th king) who had three queens; thus eight cups are placed for serving.*

Bottom: *Pouring the wine is Yi Pong-hun — eighteenth generation of the fourteenth son of Song-jong (9th king). Holding the wine cup is Yi Pong-dok — sixteenth generation of the fourth son of Chung-jong (11th king).*

Main Gate of Chongmyo Shrine

An intriguing tale is told about an event that took place in front of this gate during the reign of Chong-jo (22nd king). One day when the king was going to Chongmyo to pay respects to the spirits of his ancestors, he met a woman with a child on her back. Astounded by the young child's beauty, he asked the woman who she was. The servant answered that the child was the daughter of Kim Cho-sun. But to the king's surprise the small girl spoke up and chided the maid for answering incorrectly, telling her how the question should have been answered. "You should have told the king that I am the daughter of *sungji* (secretary to the king) Kim Cho-sun," she said in the most formal of speech. King Chong-jo then talked with the child, who always replied in the correct manner. Impressed by her alertness, he arranged to have her brought to the palace where he adopted her. Several years later, King Chong-jo betrothed this girl to Crown Prince Sun-jo. She became queen in 1800. Kim Cho-sun was from Andong, and this incident heralded the beginning of the power of the Andong Kim family, which in succeeding years hamstrung the government.

Queen Kim had two sons and three daughters. Her oldest son was named king, but died at twenty-one. When her husband passed away she acted as regent for her grandson Hon-jong (24th king), and also for Ch'ol-jong (25th king), whom she selected from a branch of the royal family banished to Kanghwa Island. Having played a lengthy and prominent role in court politics, she died at the age of sixty-eight.

This main gate of Chongmyo now has no name but once was called Ch'angyop-mun. *Ch'ang* implies progressive freshness and clarity while the character *yop* means leaves. So, Chongmyo is not a place of the dead (as is a tomb site), but is where the spirits of Yi kings continue to guide the reigning king toward a clearer and more prosperous reign.

In the later years of the Yi Dynasty the superstition of prophecy became a major concern as five hundred years drew painfully to a close. The character of *ch'ang* is written as 蒼 and can be broken down to three parts, meaning "twenty-eight rulers" (艹, double ten or twenty; 八, character for eight; 君, character for ruler). In the same manner the character for *yop* is written as 葉. Again the characters of double ten and eight are used this time in conjunction with *sei*,,which means generation, hence 28 generations of rulers. It was feared that the Yi Dynasty would end before the 28th ruler could mount the throne, therefore the gate plaque was taken down. However, this action did not influence subsequent events; Sun-jong (27th king) abdicated in 1910 and the Yi Dynasty officially came to an end.

Royal Album

King Ko-jong
26th Ruler

King Sun-jong
27the Ruler

Queen Yun
Second queen of King Sun-jong

Prepared by Japanese occupation authorities these royal portraits were used for a memorial scroll following the death of King Ko-jong in 1919.

Top Left: *The South Gate of Kyongbok Palace is seen prior to annexation when it was moved to make way for the new capitol. The twin* haet'ae *(fire-eating monster) which protected the palaces from fire are still seen in front of this reconstructed gate.*

Bottom Left: *Yi Un (Yongch'in-wang) crown prince and son of King Ko-jong poses with Princess Masako (Yi Pang-ja) following their marriage in Tokyo during April 1920. (Yi Pang-ja's private collection)*

Top Right: *Behind Kwanghwa-mun, the South Gate of Kyongbok Palace lie the central palace buildings. After annexation it was moved when the Japanese built the Government General Building (now the Capitol).*

Bottom Middle: *King Ko-jong is seated while the crown prince who later became King Sun-jong is standing. This photograph was taken of the royalty at the turn of the century.*

Bottom Right: *Om Kwibi, fifth wife of King Ko-jong was raised to the rank of queen when Yi Un her son was selected crown prince. She died in July 1911 at the age of fifty-six.*

Top: *This photograph was taken shortly after annexation. In the center is King Ko-jong wearing the royal clothing similar to the portrait in red. On King Ko-jong's left is Queen Yun, and right is Prince Yi Un (Yongch'in-wang); the baby Princess Tok-hye; King Sun-jong, eldest son of Ko-jong by Queen Min; and Prince Yi Kang (Uich'in-wang). Next to Queen Yun is Kim Ssi, senior wife of Yi Kang who remained childless and Yi Kon, eldest son of Yi Kang by another wife.*

Bottom: *This royal portrait was taken in the Toksu Palace shortly before King Ko-jong's death. From left to right: Yi Un, King Sun-jong, King Ko-jong, Queen Yun and Princess Tok-hye. (Yi Pang-ja's private collection)*

This wedding portrait of Yi Pang-ja (Princess Masako) was taken on the day of her marriage to Yi Un (Yongch'in-wang) in Tokyo, Japan, April 28, 1920.

Prince Yi Un was twenty-three and the princess twenty. Three days after celebrating their fiftieth wedding anniversary Yi Un passed away May 1, 1970 within the walls of Naksonjae. Extremely active, Princess Yi Pang-ja continues her social work in Korea with the Myong Hwee Vocational Guidance Center which she founded thirteen years previously naming it after her husband's pen name.
(Yi Pang-ja's private collection)

Top: *After the birth of Yi Chin, Yongch'in-wang visited Korea. This portrait was taken in Taejo-jon in 1922. Left to right are Princess Tok-hye, Princess Yi Pang-ja (Masako), Queen Yun, King Sun-jong, Crown Prince Yi Un and a palace attendant holding the infant son, Yi Chin. During this state visit Yi Chin mysteriously died and, as claimed by the parents, because of poisoning. (Yi Pang-ja's private collection)*

Bottom Left: *Princess Yi Pang-ja is helped by palace* sanggung *as she leaves Taejo-jon in Ch'angdok Palace during her state visit in 1922. An attendant is carrying her young son, Yi Chin. (Yi Pang-ja's private collection)*

Bottom Right: *The royal procession enters Ch'angdok Palace during Princess Yi Pang-ja's visit to Korea and audience with King Sun-jong in 1922. The royal party was coming from the Toksu Palace and riding in the cadillac now on display in the Ch'angdok Palace. (Yi Pang-ja's private collection)*

Top Left: *This royal portrait of Tok-hye was taken prior to her departure to Japan. Born in 1912 she is the last living child of King Ko-jong.*

Top Right: *Portrait of Prince Yuk born to King Ko-jong by his sixth wife, Yi Kwiin, Kwanghwa-dang was taken during the early years after annexation. Prince Yuk died after twenty months.*

Middle: *In the closing years of the dynasty King Ko-jong is seen with court attendants. Prince Yi Un is visible on the far left with court eunuchs standing beside him.*

Bottom: *Queen Yun, second wife of Sun-jong, is in the center with government officials, their wives and many court attendants. The officials in front starting from right to left are: Mr. Ko who accompanied Yi Un to Japan; Mr. Suanatsu, finance minister; Mr. Cho, Minister of Agriculture; Prime Minister; Mr. Yu, uncle of the queen; Mr. Komiya, manager of the Yi Household and an unidentified Korean official. This group picture was taken in front of the silk culture building west of Chuhap-ru within the Secret Garden.*

Top: *Young Koreans dressed in modern clothes pose in front of Naksonjae pavilions in Ch'angdok Palace. These buildings can still be seen as one enters the gate to the Secret Garden a few yards away.*

Bottom: *The ground breaking building dedication of Ch'ongdokpu, which was to be later the capitol of modern Korea is shown in this photo. Palace structures are seen beyond. Later the foundation was laid as the palace buildings and Kwanghwa Gate were demolished or removed. Capitol was completed in 1926 and was used during the occupation as the Government General Building.*

Left: *This official court picture of concubine Kim, Samch'uk-dang, was taken in 1911. She was twenty-three and a palace* sanggung *(court lady). She had recently become the official wife of King Ko-jong. On her right is* Sanggung *Han Hui-sun who was her close friend.* Han Sanggung *later became the chief palace cook and died January 5, 1972.*

Right: *Samch'uk-dang Kim Ssi died September 23, 1970. The funeral procession prepares to leave her retirement home near the Kyongbok Palace on September 27.*

Bottom: *Kwiin Kim Ssi, Samch'uk-dang, the ninth and last official wife of King Ko-jong, lived in quiet seclusion near Kyongbok Palace until her death on September 23, 1970. This photo was taken two years prior.*

Top Left: *The door to the courtyard entrance is open where Kwanghwa-dang and Samch'uk-dang, wives of the late King Kojong, lived in retirement until their deaths. These buildings were given to them by King Sun-jong.*

Top Right: *The oldest royal* sanggung *(court lady) peers into the memorial shrine for Kwanghwa-dang, wife of King Ko-jong, who passed away in 1967. On the altar is the photograph of*

*Kwiin Yi Ssi, Kwanghwa-dang.
Chong Sanggung was ninety years old at the time of this photograph. She passed away the following year.*

Bottom: *Concubine Kwanghwa-dang on May 11, 1914 received this certificate raising her to the rank of official wife of King Ko-jong. Concubines received this rank of* kwiin *after the birth of their first child. She was twenty-one and the king was fifty-five years old when Prince Yuk was born. The* tojang *(stamp seal) and signature of Ko-jong are in the upper left corner. The King's signature name was derived from the Chinese characters for the year, month and day he was born.*

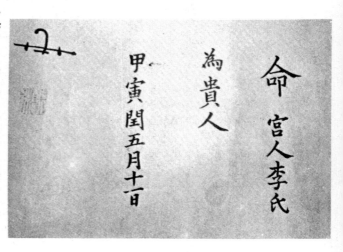

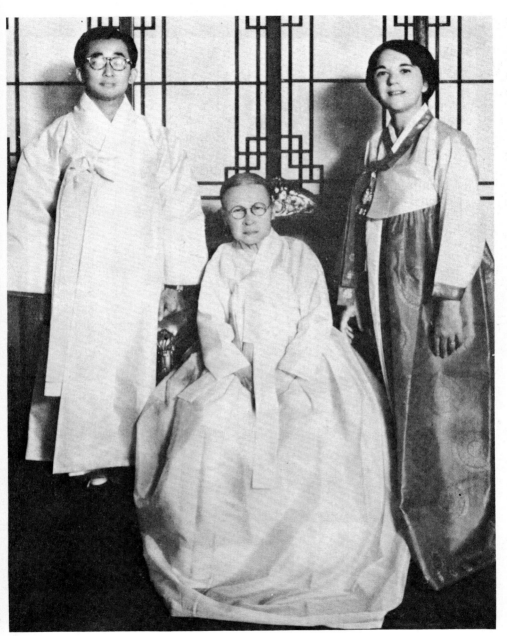

This photograph was taken in Naksonjae of Queen Yun, second wife to King Sun-jong, in June 1963. Queen Yun entered the palace in 1906 as a twelve-year-old bride of Sun-jong. In this photograph she was sixty-eight. Mr. Kyu Lee (Yi Ku), nephew of Sun-jong and his wife Julia recently arrived in Korea from the US. (Yi Pang-ja's private collection)

DESCENDANTS OF 26th KING KO-JONG

CHILDREN   SPOUSE

Queen Min (1851–1895)
(Murdered by Japanese)
(3rd wife)
- Wonja-2nd son (died after 4 days) Dec. 1871
- Daughter (died after six months) May-Nov. 1873
- Yi Sun-jong (1874–1926) 27th King
- Taegun-4th son (died early-1875)
- Taegun-6th son (died early-1878)

Queen Min—1st wife (1872–1904)
Queen Yun – 2nd wife (1894–1966)

Lady Om (1854–1911) (5th wife) — Yi Un "Yongch'in-wang" (1897–1970) 7th son of Ko-jong by concubine but later declared heir to throne. (Died May 1) — *Yi Pang-ja (Princess Masako) (1901–) (Japanese royalty)

Yi Kwiin "Yongbo-dang" (1843–1928) (1st wife) — Yi Sun "Wanhwa-gun" (1868–1880) 1st son of Ko-jong, Records indicate he died of smallpox at age of 12 (rumors say he was poisoned). Note: Friction between Taewon-gun and Queen Min began over the regent's desire to make this son the crown prince.

Yi Kwiin "Naean-dang" (1847–1914) (2nd wife)
- Daughter (died early)
- Daughter (died early)

Chang Kwiin (4th wife) — Yi Kang "Uich'in-wang" (1876–1955) 5th son of Ko-jong by concubine. Named to be king after Sung-jong. Born outside of palace because of friction between Min and Chang. — Kim Ssi "Sadang-gung" (official wife but no child)

Yi Kwiin "Kwanghwa-dang" (1885–1967) (6th wife) — Yi Yuk (died after 20 months) 8th son of Ko-jong by concubine

Yang Kwiin "Pongyong-dang" (1882–1929) (7th wife) — *Princess Tok-hye (1912–) married 1928 — Count So (Japanese noble) was governor of Tsushima

Chong Kwiin "Pohyon-dang" (1872–1904) (8th wife) — Yi U (died early) 9th son of Ko-jong by concubine

Kim Kwiin "Samch'uk-dang" (1889-1970) (9th wife) — Note: title was given to her after 1945 out of respect. Had no children

Kim Ssi "Chonghwa-dang" (?) (10th wife) — Note: No children but received title.

CHILDREN   SPOUSE   CHILDREN

Yi Chin – 1st son (died in
1922 at age one)
(there is claim that
he was poisoned)

*Yi Ku – 2nd son ———— *Julia ———— *Eugenia (Unsuk)
(has become a naturalized   (former Miss   (adopted daughter)
American citizen)   Mullock)

CHILDREN	SPOUSE	CHILDREN
Chong Ssi	*Yi Kon "Yong-gil"	1st son
Kim Hung-in "Suin-dang"	Yi U "Song-gil" (killed in Hiroshima)	2nd son
	*Yi Taek "Su-gil"	5th son
	*Yi Kon "Myong-gil"	6th son
Chong Un-sok	Yi Pang "Hung-gil"	3rd son
Cho Byong-suk	*Yi Chang "Ch'ang-gil"	4th son
Song Ssi	Yi Kwang "Hyong-gil"	7th son
Kim Chang-ui	*Yi Hyon "Kyong-gil"	8th son
Ham Ssi	*Yi Kap "Ch'ung-gil"	9th son
Hong Chong-sun	*Yi Sok "Yong-gil"	10th son
	*Yi Chong "Chong-gil"	12th son
	*Hae-ran	7th daughter
	*Hae-ryon	8th daughter
Kim Hae-su	*Yi Pom "Mun-gil"	11th son
	*Hwi-ja	6th daughter
	*Mun	9th daughter
Yi Huchun "Sudok-dang"	*Hae-han	1st daughter
	*Hae-yon	2nd daughter
Kim Chong-wan	*Hae-ch'un	3rd daughter
Pak Yong-hui	*Hae-suk	4th daughter
Kim yong-dok	*Hae-gyong	5th daughter

——————— daughter Note: Mother was hospitalized and she stayed
with father. She died following WW II.

*Still living

CH'ILGUNG SHRINE

(Seven Palace Shrines)

Memorials for Seven Concubines whose Sons
became Kings or were Named to be Kings

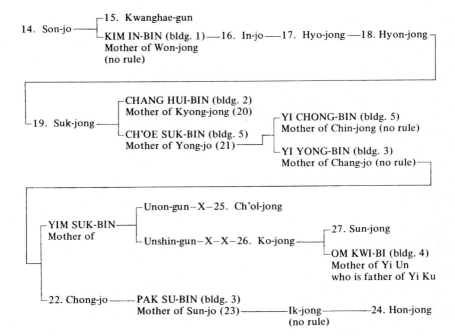

ANCESTRY CHART OF YI DYNASTY

(Synopsis of Yi Royalty, Births, Deaths and Tomb Locations)

Yi Royalty (1392–1910)	Birth and Death	Tomb Location

Note: After the name of each king is the number of years he ruled. Following each queen's family name is her posthumous name. In general conversation these two names should never be used together.

1. YI T'AE-JO (6) 1392–1398
General Yi Song-gye, 1st son of Hwan-jo by Ch'oe, ascended the throne at the age of 57 and became first dynasty king. He abdicated in favor of his 2nd son; later his 5th son took over. He had eight sons and three daughters by his two official wives. Han and Kang. He also had one daughter by concubine Yi and one daughter by concubine Hong (total: 13 children).

Nov. 5, 1335–
June 27, 1408

Konwon-Nung
(E-9 Tombs)

HAN, Shin-ui (raised to Queen posthumously)
Had six sons and two daughters. Second and fifth became kings.

1337–
Oct. 29, 1391

Che-Nung
(north Korea)

KANG, Shin-dok (2nd Queen)
Had two sons and one daughter. Sons were involved in subversion against their father. Tomb was originally at Chong-dong but moved in 1409 by T'ae-jong.

Died
Oct. 3, 1396

Chong-Nung
(near East Gate)

2. YI CHONG-JONG (2) 1398–1400
Second son of Yi T'ae-jo by Queen Han, abdicated in favor of brother, 5th son of T'ae-jo. Had fifteen sons and eight daughters by concubines (Chi-3 sons & 1 daughter, Mun-1 son, Yi-1 son, Yun-4 sons & 1 daughter, Chi-2 sons, Ki-4 sons & 1 daughter, 5 daughters-unknown, total: 23 children).

July 26, 1357–
Oct. 24, 1419

Hu-Nung
(north Korea)

KIM, Chong-an (Queen)
Had no children.

Jan. 30, 1355–
Aug. 11, 1412

Hu-Nung
(north Korea)

3. YI T'AE-JONG (18) 1400–1418
Fifth son of T'ae-jo by Queen Han, had four sons by Queen Min and eight sons by five concubines. Also had four daughters by Min and thirteen daughters by seven concubines (Shin-3 sons & 6 daughters, Ahn-1 son & 2 daughters, Ahn-1 son, Kim-1 son, Kim-1 daughter, Ch'oe-2 sons, Kwon-1 daughter, No-1 daughter, Yi-1 daughter, 1 daughter-unknown, total: 29 children). He was an energetic reformer. Retired in favor of his 3rd son and died in 1422. Tomb has twice the usual number of statues.

June 21, 1367–
June 9, 1422

Hon-Nung
(Kwangju)

Yi Royalty	Birth and Death	Tomb Location
MIN, Won'g-yong (Queen) Had four sons and four daughters. First son was Yang-nyong, 2nd son was Hyo-nyong and 3rd son became Se-jong. Fourth son was Song-nyong.	Aug. 6, 1365 Aug. 27, 1420	Hon-Nung (Kwangju)
SHIN Shin-bin (concubine) Had three sons and six daughters.	unknown	unknown
4. YI SE-JONG (32) 1418–1450 Known as the Alphabet King, he was third son of T'ae-jong. Had eight sons by Queen Shim and ten sons by three concubines (Kim-6, Yang-3, Kang-1). Had two daughters by Queen Shim and one daughter by Song and Yi (total: 22 children). Desired to have simple tomb. Tomb originally next to T'ae-jong's but moved to Yoju in 1469.	May 15, 1397– Apr. 8, 1450	Yong-Nung (Yoju)
SHIM, So-hon (Queen) Had eight sons and two daughters.	Oct. 20, 1395– Apr. 28, 1446	Yong-Nung (Yoju)
KIM Shin-bin (concubine) Had six sons.	July 12, 1406– Sept. 4, 1465	Shinbin-Myo (west of Suwon)
YANG Hye-bin (concubine) Had three sons and also raised grandson Tan-jong, his mother, Kwon, having died in childbirth. She was exiled by King Se-jo and died shortly thereafter.	unknown	unknown
5. YI MUN-JONG (2) 1450–1452 Se-jong's 1st son who supposedly died of grief after his father's death. His first two wives (Kim and Pong) were exiled. Had one son and two daughters by Queen Kwon and concubine Yang. Kwon's daughter Kyong-hae (Tan-jong's sister) was exiled, bore a son, later killed by Se-jo, as was her husband. Her son became famous governor, Chong Mi-su.	Nov. 24, 1414– June 11, 1452	Hyon-Nung (E-9 Tombs)
KWON, Hyon-dok (raised to Queen posthumously) Third wife of Mun-jong, the 1st two having been exiled. At age 23 she bore Tan-jong and died in childbirth. First buried near Suwon (So-Nung) but *nung* title removed by Se-jo in 1458. She was buried at E-9 Tombs in 1531.	Apr. 26, 1418– Aug. 19, 1441	Hyon-Nung (E-9 Tombs)
6. YI TAN-JONG (3) 1452–1455 Prince Yi Hong-wi, first son of Mun-jong, became king at age 11. Forced to abdicate and eventually killed by uncle (King Se-jo). His tomb originally titled Nosangun-Myo, raised to *nung* by King Suk-jong. No children.	Aug. 18, 1441– Nov. 19, 1457	Chang-Nung (Yongwol)

Yi Royalty	Birth and Death	Tomb Location

SONG, Chong-sun (Queen)
Lived to be 81 and died during the reign of 11th king. Had no children. She became a nun after Tan-jong was exiled and stayed at Ch'ongyong-Sa, a temple just outside the East Gate. Later she lived with Chong Mi-su, son of her husband's older sister, and is now buried near their ancestral graves. Tomb was raised to *nung* in 1699 by King Suk-jong.

1440–
July 17, 1521

Sa-Nung
(near Kumgok)

7. YI SE-JO (13) 1455–1468
After killing his nephew, Tan-jong, this second son of Se-jong became one of the greater Yi Dynasty rulers. Had two sons by Queen Yun and two sons by concubine Pak. (Only had one daughter by queen.) Retired in favor of 2nd son Ye-jong.

Nov. 16, 1417–
Oct. 1, 1468

Kwang-Nung
(National Forest Reserve)

YUN, Chong-hi (Queen)
Had two sons, oldest being Tok-jong, second son became King Ye-jong. Queen also had one daughter.

Dec. 17, 1418–
May 15, 1483

Kwang-Nung
(National Forest Reserve)

YI TOK-JONG (raised to King posthumously)
This oldest son of Se-jo died mysteriously at the age of 19, fifty days before Tan-jong was murdered in Yongwol. Though he never ruled, his tomb was given the title of *nung*. Had two sons and one daughter by Han. His second son became 9th King.

Oct. 12, 1438–
Sept. 29, 1457

Kyong-Nung
(W-5 Tombs)

HAN, So-hui (raised to Queen posthumously)
Lived almost 50 years longer than her husband. She had two sons, the second becoming Song-jong (9th king). Toksu Palace was originally built for her first son, Prince Wol-san. Han also had one daughter.

Oct. 16, 1437–
May 21, 1504

Kyong-Nung
(W-5 Tombs)

8. YI YE-JONG (1) 1468–1469
Prince Ha-yang, 2nd son of Se-jo, came to the throne at age 18. His mother Queen Yun was regent for both eighth and ninth kings. Had two sons and one daughter but because of the political power of Queen Yun neither son became king.

Jan. 23, 1450–
Jan. 9, 1469

Ch'ang-Nung
(W-5 Tombs)

HAN, Chang-sun (raised to Queen posthumously)
Died, before her husband became king, at the age of 17. Her younger sister became the queen of 9th king but also died in her teens. She had only one son.

Mar. 3, 1445–
Jan. 14, 1462

Kong-Nung
(Paju)

HAN, An-sun (2nd Queen)
Had only one son and one daughter.

Died
Feb. 12, 1499

Ch'ang-Nung
(W-5 Tombs)

Yi Royalty	Birth and Death	Tomb Location
9. YI SONG-JONG (26) 1469–1495	Aug. 28, 1457–	Son-Nung
This second son of Tok-jong came to the throne at the age of 12, with Queen Yun (Se-jo) as regent. Queen Yun and Han (Tok-jong's wife) were powerful enough to place Song-jong on the throne rather than the oldest son of Ye-jong. Song-jong had 15 sons by seven concubines and one son by Queen Yun (Chong–hyon). Had one daughter by queen and eleven by six concubines (Yun-1 son, Hong-7 sons & 3 daughters, Shim-2 sons & 2 daughters, Kim-1 son, Kim-3 daughters, Chong-2 sons & 1 daughter, Kwon-1 son, Kwon-1 daughter, Ha-1 son, Om-1 daughter, total: 28 children). Upon the death of Queen Han, Yun (Pop-yong) was raised from the rank of concubine to queen. Yun's (Pop-yong) son was Prince Yonsan-gun, and she was later banished and poisoned.	Jan. 29, 1495	(Kwangju)
HAN, Kong-hui (1st Queen)	Nov. 17, 1456–	Sun-Nung
Did not have any children.	May 9, 1474	(Paju)
YUN, Pop-yong (2nd Queen–banished)	Died 1483	Hoe-Myo
She was mother of Yonsan-gun and, because of her temper, was banished when the boy was four. Three years later she was condemned to take poison. Yonsan-gun became crown prince at the age of eight.		(originally near Kyonghee Univ. Oct. 25, '69 moved to So-Sam-Nung)
YUN, Chong-hyon (3rd Queen)	July 31, 1462–	Son-Nung
Mother of 11th king. She had only one son and one daughter.	Sept. 23, 1530	(Kwangju)
HONG Suk-bin (concubine)	unknown	unknown
Had seven sons and three daughters.		
10. YONSAN-GUN (11) 1495–1506 (banished)	Nov. 11, 1476–	Yonsan-Myo
Instigated a reign of terror and misrule. Spent much of his time avenging his mother's death. His reign was ended by a revolt led by Pak Won-jong, the younger brother of Pak Sun-jun, 2nd wife of Prince Wol-san. Yonsan-gun had taken her for his wife and she had killed herself: thus her brother sought revenge.	Nov. 6, 1506	(located near Uidong)
SHIN, Yonsan-bi (Queen)	unknown	Yonsan-Myo
Yonsan-gun had only one queen but a rumored 3000 concubines.		(located near Uidong)
11. CHUNG-JONG (38) 1506–1544	Apr. 25, 1488–	Chong-Nung
This prince was 2nd son of Song-jong by his 3rd Queen Yun (Chong-hyon). His was a golden age. Had two sons and five daughters by queens and seven sons and six daughters by six concubines. (Pak-1 son & 2 daughters, Ahn-2 sons & 1 daughter, Hong-2 sons, Hong-1 son, Yi-1 son & 2 daughters,	Dec. 9, 1544	(Kwangju)

Yi Royalty	Birth and Death	Tomb Location

Kim-1 daughter, total: 20 children). His tomb was originally at Hui-Nung but was moved near his father's tomb in 1562 by his third queen.

SHIN, Tan-gyong (1st Queen)
Was divorced and banished at age nineteen one week after marriage because father had been intimate with Yonsan-gun. Tomb was raised to *nung* in 1739 by Yong-jo (21st king). Had no children and lived to the age of 71.

Feb. 16, 1487 –
Jan. 6, 1558

On-Nung
(near Uijongbu)

YUN, Chang-gyong (2nd Queen)
Died six days after giving birth to a boy who became In-jong (12th king). Also had one daughter. Tomb originally near T'ae-jong's tomb but moved in 1537.

Aug. 19, 1491 –
Mar. 26, 1515

Hui-Nung
(W-3 Tombs)

YUN, Mun-jong (3rd Queen)
She was mother of Myong-jong (13th king) and gave birth also to four daughters. She was extremely powerful and her tomb is typical of a king's. Moved her husband's original tomb near his second wife to a site near Song-jong's, expecting to be buried there also. However, she was buried near her son.

Dec. 12, 1501 –
May 10, 1565

T'ae-Nung
(near Military Academy)

YI Ssi (concubine)
This concubine became Chung-jong's wife as result of a dream he had concerning her before they met. She had no children.

unknown

unknown

AHN Chang-bin (concubine)
Had two sons and one daughter. Her second son was Chung-jong's last and 9th son. Tok-hung Taewon-gun, who became the father of Son-jo (14th king).

July 1499 –
Oct. 1554

Changbin-Myo
(within National Cemetery)

12. YI IN-JONG (1) 1544–1545
In-jong died either of grief over his father Chung-jong's death or poison administered by his stepmother, Yun (Mun-jong) who wanted her own son king. Family feud between 2nd wife Yun and 3rd wife Yun resulted in countless deaths. In-jong had no children.

Mar. 20, 1515 –
Aug. 17, 1545

Hyo-Nung
(W-3 Tombs)

PAK, In-song (Queen)
Lived more than thirty years past her husband's death. She had no children.

Oct. 28, 1514
Jan. 16, 1578

Hyo-Nung
(W-3 Tombs)

13. YI MYONG-JONG (22) 1545–1567
He was second son of King Chung-jong by Queen Yun (3rd wife). Came to the throne at the age of 11 with Yun (Mun-jong) as regent. He had only one son and no daughter by queen, but before his death he requested that his nephew Son-jo become king.

July 13, 1534 –
Aug. 12, 1567

Kang-Nung
(near Military Academy)

Yi Royalty	Birth and Death	Tomb Location

SHIM, In-sun (Queen)
Regent for her nephew, who became King Son-jo.

July 7, 1532–
Feb. 22, 1575

Kang-Nung
(near Military Academy)

14. YI SON-JO (41) 1567–1608
Prince Ha-sung came to the throne at the age of 15. He was the 3rd son of Tok-hung Taewon-gun and nephew of Myong-jong. He had thirteen sons and ten daughters by his six concubines, and one son and one daughter by Queen Kim (In-mok). (Kim-2 sons, Kim-4 sons & 5 daughters, Kim-1 son, Han-3 sons and 1 daughter, Min-2 sons & 3 daughters, Hong-1 son & 1 daughter, total: 25 children). His reign saw formation of political factions and invasion by Hideyoshi in 1592.

Dec. 6, 1552–
Mar. 16, 1608

Mok-Nung
(E-9 Tombs)

PAK, U-in (1st Queen)
Lived to be 45 but died childless.

May 15, 1555–
Aug. 1, 1600

Mok-Nung
(E-9 Tombs)

KIM, In-mok (2nd Queen)
Had one daughter and one son born two years before Son-jo's death. Kwanghae-gun, son of concubine Kim Kong-bin, had already been named crown prince. Fearful of the boy's claim to the throne Kwanghae-gun killed him after he had been exiled to Kanghwa Island by overheating his *ondol* room. The boy was only six.

Dec. 15, 1584
Aug. 13, 1632

Mok-Nung
(E-9 Tombs)

KIM In-bin (concubine)
She was the mother of Won-jong, who was the fifth son of Son-jo. Why he was not also killed is a mystery. Kim In-bin had four sons and five daughters. Won-jong's son later became 16th king.

Feb. 1555–
Oct. 29, 1613

Sunkang-Won
(near Kwang-Nung)

KIM Kong-bin (concubine)
Had two sons, Imhae-gun and Kwanghae-gun. When Kwanghae-gun became king he had his older brother killed. Kim's tomb was given the title of Song-Nung but title was taken away by In-jo (16th king).

Oct. 11, 1553–
May 11, 1578

Song-Myo
(near Kumgok)

15. YI KWANGHAE-GUN (15) 1608–1623
(banished)
Second son of Son-jo by concubine Kim Kong-bin. Later banished and not recognized as king. Older brother Imhae-gun was passed over as crown prince because he was too wild. Imhae-gun was killed by order of Kwanghae-gun.

Nov. 1573–
Aug. 1641

Kwanghae-Myo
(near Kumgok)

YU, Mun-hwa (Queen)
A most unhappy woman who once said that if she returned to this life after death she prayed that it would not be as a queen.

Died Oct. 1623

Kwanghae-Myo
(near Kumgok)

Yi Royalty	Birth and Death	Tomb Location

YI WON-JONG (raised to King posthumously)
Did not rule, but his tomb was raised to rank of king. He was 5th son of Son-jo and 3rd son by Kim In-bin. Tomb was originally at Yang-ju, moved in 1627 and raised to *nung* in 1632. Won-jong had four sons (one son by concubine Kim) with the eldest becoming King In-jo in 1622. Had no daughters.

Aug. 12, 1580–
Feb. 1, 1620

Chang-Nung
(Kimpo)

KU, In-hon (raised to Queen posthumously)
Had three sons. Eldest was In-jo.

June 3, 1578
Feb. 11, 1626

Chang-Nung
(Kimpo)

16. YI IN-JO (26) 1623–1649
Prince Nung-yang, the eldest son of Won-jong, was the nephew of Kwanghae-gun and grandson of Son-jo. His reign marked the lowest point of the Yi period. He was the builder of South Fortress. His sons were hostages in China from 1637 until 1645. In-jo had five sons by Queen Han and two sons and one daughter by concubine Cho. Tomb was moved to Chang-Nung in 1731 by Yong-jo (21st king).

Dec. 7, 1595–
June 17, 1649

Chang-Nung
(near Munsan)

HAN, In-yol (1st Queen)
Mother of five sons and no daughters. The older sons were carried to China following the Manchu invasion.

Aug. 16, 1594–
Jan. 16, 1636

Chang-Nung
(near Munsan)

CHO, Chang-yol (2nd Queen)
Had no children.

Dec. 16, 1624–
Sept. 20, 1688

Hui-Nung
(E-9 Tombs)

CHO Kwiin (concubine)
She had two sons and one daughter by king. Is not to be confused with Queen Cho.

unknown

unknown

17. YI HYO-JONG (10) 1649–1659
Prince Pong-im was made heir after the death of the crown prince, which was reputedly caused by King In-jo, who preferred his second son. His tomb is near King Se-jong's, whom he greatly admired. He had one son and six daughters by his queen and one daughter by concubine Yi Ahn-bin. During his reign, *Sparwehl* wrecked on Cheju Island and sailor Hendrick Hamel eventually escaped to Holland and wrote a book about Korea.

July 4, 1619–
June 23, 1659

Yong-Nung
(Yoju)'

CHANG, In-son (Queen)
Mother of 18th king, who was only son of Hyo-jong. She is buried in front and to the right of Hyo-jong.

Feb. 9, 1619–
Mar. 31, 1674

Yong-Nung
(Yoju)

YI Ahn-bin (concubine)
Had only one daughter by king.

Sept. 1622–
Oct. 23, 1693

Ahnbin-Myo
(near Kwanghae-gun's tomb, Kumgok)

Yi Royalty	Birth and Death	Tomb Location
18. YI HYON-JONG (15) 1659–1674 Great reformer with help of prime minister Song Shi-yol (Bismarck of Korea). King died at 33 and had only one son, who became King Suk-jong. Also had three daughters by the queen. He was born outside of Korea while father was captive in Manchuria.	Mar. 14, 1641– Sept. 18, 1674	Sung-Nung (E-9 Tombs)
KIM, Myong-song (Queen) Had one son and three daughters. Was mother of Suk-jong.	June 14, 1642– Jan. 21, 1684	Sung-Nung (E-9 Tombs)
19. YI SUK-JONG (46) 1674–1720 Prince Myong-bo started his reign at the age of 14 during the maelstrom of party strife. He was builder of the North Fortress. Suk-jong had six sons by his concubines, Chang-2, Ch'oe-3 and Pak-1. Had two daughters by Queen Kim.	Oct. 7, 1660– July 12, 1720	Myong-Nung (W-5 Tombs)
KIM, In-gyong (1st Queen) Queen ruled for only six years and died at 19 in childbirth. Had two daughters.	Oct. 25, 1661– Dec. 16, 1680	Ik-Nung (W-5 Tombs)
MIN, In-hyon (2nd Queen) Had no children but considered one of the finest queens of Korea. She was banished by the king, who favored concubine Chang, but was later reinstated. She died of boils inflicted, it is claimed, by Chang through witchcraft.	May 15, 1667– Sept. 16, 1701	Myong-Nung (W-5 Tombs)
KIM, In-won (3rd Queen) Also had no child. Tomb is above and to the left of the king's, which is unique.	Nov. 3, 1687– May 13, 1757	Myong-Nung (W-5 Tombs)
CHANG Hui-bin (concubine) Mother of Kyong-jong (20th king). She caused terrible strife in the courts which culminated in the murder of Song Shi-yol and banishment of Queen Min (1689). Deeds finally discovered and Chang was condemned to take poison. She was considered very beautiful. Had two sons.	Died-1701	Chang Huibin-Myo (moved to So-O-Nung Dec. 11, 1970)
CH'OE Suk-bin (concubine) Mother of Yong-jo, who later became 21st king. Yong-jo was the second of three sons by Ch'oe Suk-bin.	Nov. 6, 1670– Mar. 9, 1718	Soryong-Won (Paju)
20. YI KYONG-JONG (4) 1720–1724 Son of concubine Chang. He was feebleminded and constantly ill because of an injury inflicted by his angry mother on the way to her execution. He became sterile because of this injury.	Nov. 20, 1688– Oct. 11, 1724	In-Nung (near Kyonghee Univ.)
SHIM, Tan-i (raised to Queen posthumously) Died at the age of 32 before her husband became king.	July 11, 1686– Mar. 8, 1718	Hye-Nung (E-9 Tombs)

Yi Royalty	Birth and Death	Tomb Location

O, Son-i (2nd Queen)
Her family name means "fish." She died at the age of 25.

Dec. 14, 1705 – Aug. 12, 1730

In-Nung (near Kyonghee Univ.)

21. YI YONG-JO (52) 1724–1776
Fourth son of King Suk-jong, he was half brother of Kyong-jong by concubine Ch'oe. There were brilliant reforms during early period of reign. At age 68 in a rage he accused the crown prince, Sa-do, his only son, of revolt and killed him by suffocation in a rice box. He had no children by his two queens but he had two sons and 12 daughters by four concubines (Yi-1 son & 2 daughters, Yi-1 son & 6 daughters, Mun-2 daughters, Cho-2 daughters, total: 14 children). He died at 82 and ruled 52 years, longer than any other Yi Dynasty king.

Oct. 12, 1694 – Apr. 22, 1776

Won-Nung (E-9 Tombs)

SO, Chong-song (1st Queen)
She died at 64, but her husband, Yong-jo, lived 19 years longer and married again. She had no children. The tomb faces west rather than south, and there is space reserved for Yong-jo which is still vacant, since he is buried with his second queen.

Jan. 12, 1693 – Apr. 3, 1757

Hong-Nung (W-5 Tombs)

KIM, Chong-sun (2nd Queen)
She was a girl of 12 when she married Yong-jo who was then 63. She lived to help place Sun-jo (23rd king) on the throne.

Dec. 3, 1745 – Feb. 11, 1805

Won-Nung (E-9 Tombs)

YI Chong-bin (concubine)
She was mother of Chin-jong, who was first son of Yong-jo. Chin-jong was named crown prince but died early. Also she had two daughters.

1694 – Nov. 16, 1721

Won'gil-Won (Paju)

YI Yong-bin (concubine)
She was mother of Chang-jo (Prince Sa-do) and died two years after her son, the crown prince, was killed by the king. She had six daughters and one son. Princess Hwahwah, the last of her daughters and ninth of Yong-jo's, hated her brother Prince Sa-do and it is believed suggested the method of execution which killed her brother.

July 18, 1696 – July 26, 1764

Wan'gyong-Won (formally at Yonsei Univ., moved to So-O-Nung Sept. 8, 1970.)

MUN So-ui (concubine)
She had two daughters of her own. She plotted to falsify having a son, who would have been made crown prince, but plot failed. She also hated Prince Sa-do and she was later banished by Chong-jo (22nd king) and died in exile.

unknown

unknown

YI CHIN-JONG (raised to King posthumously)
Was named to be king but died at the age of nine. He was first son of Yong-jo by Yi Chong-bin. Tomb was raised to *nung* by Ko-jong (26th king).

Apr. 5, 1719 Nov. 17, 1728

Yong-Nung (Paju)

Yi Royalty	Birth and Death	Tomb Location
CHO, Hyo-sun (raised to Queen posthumously) She married when the prince was nine and she was twelve. She had no children.	Jan. 8, 1716 Nov. 14, 1751	Yong-Nung (Paju)
YI CHANG-JO (raised to King posthumously) Prince Sa-do was second son of Yong-jo and was named to be king upon death of Chin-jong. At 27, he was accused of revolt and though innocent was placed in a rice box until he died. He had two sons and two daughters by Hong, three sons and one daughter by concubines (Yim-2 sons, Pak-1 son & 1 daughter). His second son by Hong was ten years old at the time of the father's murder, and later became 22nd king. Tomb was erected in 1785 and made *nung* in 1899 by Ko-jong.	Feb. 13, 1735 July 12, 1762	Yung-Nung (Suwon)
HONG, Hyon-gyong (raised to Queen posthumously) The mother of Prince Ui-so and Chong-jo; also had two daughters. Lived to be over eighty. She wrote a book about Prince Sa-do, *Han Chungrok,* when she was sixty.	Aug. 6, 1735– Jan. 13, 1816	Yung-Nung (Suwon)
YIM Suk-bin (concubine) This concubine had two sons who began a generation of later kings. Her first son was Unon-gun, who was the grandfather of the 25th king, Ch'ol-jong. Her second son was Unshin-gun, who was the great-grandfather of Ko-jong (26th king).	unknown	unknown
22. YI CHONG-JO (24) 1776-1800 Chong-jo was 2nd son of Chang-jo, who was murdered by King Yong-jo. In 1785 Suwon was considered for his new capital. Persecution against the church started in 1791 (est. six thousand Christians in Korea). The king had three sons and one daughter, all by concubines. Prince Mun-hyo was crown prince but died early (age four). Dowager Kim (Yong-jo's queen) placed Sun-jo, second son of king by concubine Pak, on the throne.	Oct. 28, 1752– Aug. 18, 1800	Kon-Nung (Suwon)
KIM, Hyo-i (Queen) Had no children.	Jan. 5, 1754 Apr. 10, 1821	Kon-Nung (Suwon)
PAK Su-bin (concubine) Had one son and one daughter. Her son became Sun-jo (23rd king) upon the death of the crown prince by concubine Song Ui-bin.	May 8, 1770 Dec. 26, 1822	Hwigyong-Won (near Kwang-Nung)
SONG Ui-bin (concubine) Had two sons, 1st and 3rd sons of Chong-jo. Her first son was made crown prince but died early.	July 8, 1753– 1789	Uibin-Myo (W-3 Tombs)
23. YI SUN-JO (34) 1800–1834 He was second son of Chong-jo and became king at the age of 10. Dowager Kim, widow of	July 27, 1790– Dec. 13, 1834	In-Nung (Kwangju)

Yi Royalty	Birth and Death	Tomb Location

Yong-jo, ruled as regent. King Sun-jo and all succeeding kings began their reigns with regents, since they were under age. Visit by first Protestant missionary, Gutzlaff, by ship from China. Tomb originally at Paju and moved in 1856. Had two sons who died early and three daughters by queen. One daughter by concubine Pak Suk-ui.

KIM, Sun-won (Queen) — June 9, 1789– / Oct. 1, 1857 — In-Nung (Kwangju)
Queen was from Andong area, and family later held great power. She had two sons and three daughters by the king. Mother of Ik-jong.

IK-JONG (raised to King posthumously) — Sept. 18, 1809– / June 25, 1830 — Su-Nung (E-9 Tombs)
Prince Mun-jo married at age 11 and died at 21. He was 1st son of Sun-jo and father of Hon-jong. Ik-jong had only one son and no daughters.

CHO, Shin-jong (raised to Queen posthumously) — Jan. 21, 1809– / June 4, 1890 — Su-Nung (E-9 Tombs)
She was mother of Hon-jong (24th king) and was later responsible for placing Ko-jong, son of Hung-son Taewon-gun, on the throne in 1864. Lived to be 81.

24. YI HON-JONG (15) 1834–1849 — Sept. 8, 1827– / July 25, 1849 — Kyong-Nung (E-9 Tombs)
He came to the throne at the age of seven with Kim Sun-won (wife of Sun-jo) as regent. First Western resident missionary came to Seoul, crossing the Yalu River in 1835, and others soon followed. All executed at Yongsan 1839. Hon-jong had one daughter by concubine Kim Suk-ui and no sons. He died at age 22 due to venereal disease.

KIM, Hyo-hyon (1st Queen) — Apr. 27, 1828– / Oct. 18, 1843 — Kyong-Nung (E-9 Tombs)
Also from the Andong Kims, she died at the age of 15. No children.

HONG, Hyo-jong (2nd Queen) — Mar. 7, 1831– / Feb. 17, 1904 — Kyong-Nung (E-9 Tombs)
Married to the king at age thirteen and lived to be 73. One of three dynasty queens to live into the 20th century. No children.

KIM Kyong-bin (concubine) — Aug. 27, 1832 / 1908 — Kyongbin-Myo (W-3 Tombs)
Became concubine of king before the age of 14. Had no children but was an obvious favorite, since Naksonjae was built for her by order of king in 1846.

KIM Suk-ui (concubine) — Jan. 10, 1813– / Nov. 12, 1886 — Sukui-Myo (W-3 Tombs)
Was 14 years the king's senior. She produced Hon-jong's one and only child (daughter).

25. YI CH'OL-JONG (15) 1849–1864 — July 25, 1831– / Jan. 16, 1864 — Ye-Nung (W-3 Tombs)
When King Hon-jong died without heir, regent Kim (wife of Sun-jo) nominated a boy of 18 to be king. He was born on Kanghwa Island and was

Yi Royalty	Birth and Death	Tomb Location

grandson of Unon-gun, half brother of Chong-jo (22nd king). His great-grandmother was Yim Suk-bin, concubine of Prince Sa-do (Chang-jo). Ch'ol-jong was third son of Chon-gye Taewon-gun by concubine Yom. The king had one son by Queen Kim, four sons and six daughters by concubines (Pak-1 son & 1 daughter, Cho-2 sons, Yi-1 son & 1 daughter, Pang-2 daughters, Kim-1 daughter, Pom-1 daughter, total: 11 children). With the exception of one daughter by Pom who died shortly after marriage, they all died early.

	Birth and Death	Tomb Location
KIM, Ch'ol-lin (Queen)	Apr. 27, 1837–	Ye-Nung
Queen Kim was also from Andong and had one son, who died before her husband's death.	June 29, 1878	(W-3 Tombs)

26. YI KO-JONG (43) 1864–1907 — Sept. 8, 1852 / Jan. 21, 1919 — Hong-Nung (Kumgok)

Queen dowager Cho (wife of Ik-jong) took state seals and declared new king, second son of Hung-son Taewon-gun. Boy was 12 years old and great-grandson of Unshin-gun. Unshin-gun was son of Prince Sa-do (Chang-jo) by concubine Yim Suk-bin. Ko-jong abdicated in 1907 and died at 67, having prepared his tomb in 1899. In 1866 came the great persecution of the church. He had four sons and one daughter by the queen (all but one son died early) and five sons and three daughters by seven concubines (Yi-1 son, Yi-2 daughters, Chang-1 son, Om-1 son, Yang-1 daughter, Yi-1 son, Chong-1 son, total: 13 children).

	Birth and Death	Tomb Location
MIN, Myong-song (Queen)	Nov. 17, 1851–	Hong-Nung
Mother of Sun-jong (second son of a family of four sons and one daughter) who was 44 at the time of her murder by the Japanese and Hung-son Taewon-gun. Queen Min was third wife of Ko-jong, but first queen. Tomb located originally on way to Uidong and upon death of her husband moved to Hong-Nung.	Oct. 8, 1895	(Kumgok)
YI Yongbo-dang (concubine)	Feb. 14, 1843–	Kwiin-Myo
First wife of Ko-jong who was nine years his senior. Had one son when Ko-jong was 16, Prince Wanhwa-gun, who died at the age of 12 (1868-1880).	Nov. 6, 1928	(W-3 Tombs)
YI Naean-dang (concubine)	1847–	Kwiin-Myo
Second wife of Ko-jong and had two daughters.	Jan. 9, 1914	(W-3 Tombs)
CHANG Ssi (concubine)	unknown	Chang Ssi-Myo
Fourth wife of Ko-jong had a son Yi Kang (Uich'in-wang), who died in 1955.		(near W-3 Tombs)

Yi Royalty	Birth and Death	Tomb Location

OM Kwibi (Noble Lady)
    Fifth wife of Ko-jong was mother of Yi Un (Yongch'in-wang), who would have been 28th king. Yi Un was born in 1897, married Princess Masako of Japanese royalty, and died in 1970. Yi Un's first child died in infancy and his 2nd son is Yi Ku.

Nov. 5, 1854 –
July 20, 1911

Yonghwi-Won (on way to Uidong)

YI Kwanghwa-dang (concubine)
    Born in 1885, became a *sanggung* at age 14 and won Ko-jong's favor at 22. Had one son, Prince Yuk, who lived only 20 months. She recently died at the age of 82.

1885 –
Nov. 10, 1967

Kwiin-Myo (near Hong-Nung at Kumgok)

YANG Pongyong-dang (concubine)
    Seventh wife of Ko-jong had a daughter, Princess Tok-hye, born in 1912 and still living in Korea.

Sept. 27, 1882 –
Apr. 22, 1929

Kwiin-Myo (W-3 Tombs)

CHONG Pohyon-dang (concubine)
    Had one prince, Yi U, who died early in life.

1872 –
1904

Kwiin-Myo (grave unmarked) (W-3 Tombs)

KIM Samch'uk-dang (concubine)
    Title was given by King Sun-jong after her husband's death, though she had no children. She died at the age of 81.

1889 –
Sept. 23, 1970

Kwiin-Myo (near Hong-Nung at Kumgok)

KIM Chonghwa-dang (concubine)
    Had no children but for political reasons held high rank. King Ko-jong did not want her.

unknown

Kwiin-Myo (grave unmarked) (W-3 Tombs)

27. YI SUN-JONG (3) 1907–1910
    Second son of Ko-jong by Queen Min. Forced to abdicate by Japanese. Since he had no heir his younger half-brother Yi Un, was made heir.

Mar. 25, 1874
Apr. 25, 1926

Yu-Nung (Kumgok)

MIN, Sun-myong (1st Queen)
    Tomb was moved here on death of Sun-jong.

Nov. 20, 1872 –
Dec. 11, 1904

Yu-Nung (Kumgok)

YUN, Sun-jong (2nd Queen)
    Was buried to left of king (facing mound) in the same mound, which had never been done before. She entered the palace in 1906 as a 12-year-old bride of Sun-jong, then 23. This was two years after Queen Min's death.

Aug. 20, 1894 –
Feb. 3, 1966

Yu-Nung (Kumgok)

YI UI-MIN (named King)
    Prince Yi Un, (Yongch'in-wang) seventh son of Ko-jong by Om Kwibi, was given the rank of crown prince when Sun-jong came to the throne in 1907 since the king had no children. He was married to Princess Masako (Yi Pang-ja) in 1920. Their first son Yi Chin died in 1922 while visiting Korea. Their second son Yi Ku is precently living in Japan. Yi Un lived most of his life in Japan and returned to Korea in 1964, quietly passing away at Naksonjae at age 73.

Oct. 20, 1897
May 1, 1970

Yong-Won (Kumgok)

National Treasures
(Kukbo: First Rank)
Located in the Palaces

(Note: Designation dates are given in parentheses)

1. NT #60   Celadon Incense Burner with Lion Cover
             Location: National Museum, Seoul
             Period: Koryo Dynasty, 12th century

During the 12th century the development of celadon reached its peak. Chinese visitors praised Koryo celadon as being the best in the world. During this period animal shaped objects were popular and this incense burner is typical. The lion is hollow inside so that the smoke comes out of its mouth. Celadon objects of this period were noted for their deep greenish tones. (Oct 18, 1939)

2. NT #61   Celadon Water Ewer in the Form of a Fish Dragon
             Location: National Museum, Seoul
             Period: Koryo Dynasty, 12th century

Of all celadon pieces this object has the strangest design. Having the head of a dragon and body of a fish, this vessel has a base shaped with a lotus design. The image is similar to one of the *chapsang* figures found on roof ridges to frighten away fire and evil spirits. (Oct. 18, 1939)

3. NT #78   Gilt Bronze Seated Maitreya (Miruk) Bodhisattva
             Location: National Museum, Seoul
             Period: Three Kingdoms, 6th century

This statue, acquired in 1912 from a dealer, is a masterpiece attributed to an early Silla sculptor. Its origin and background are unknown. The square-jawed face is characterized by a hint of a smile. The right leg is lifted and crossed, while the hand is placed against the face in a meditative pose. It is one of the most important images of the Three Kingdoms era. (Dec. 2, 1959)

4. NT #79   Gold Seated Buddha from Kuhwang-ni, Kyongju
             Location: National Museum, Seoul
             Period: Silla Dynasty, 706

This image of pure gold was made in three parts, the image, base and *mandorla,* which can be separated. This slightly smiling Buddha was found with NT # 80 in 1943 within a *sari* box of a three-storied pagoda at Hwangbok temple site in Kyongju. It was recorded that this box was placed within the stone pagoda during the fifth year of Song-dok (33rd Silla king). (May 22, 1958)

5. NT #80   Gold Standing Buddha from Kuhwang-ni, Kyongju
                 Location: National Museum, Seoul
                 Period: Silla Dynasty, 706

This Buddha made of pure gold was found with NT #79 in 1943. With hair unusually high and cheeks fat, this image also has a slight smile. (Dec. 2, 1959)

6. NT #81   Stone Standing Maitreya (Miruk) Bodhisattva from Kamsan-sa Site
                 Location: National Museum, Seoul
                 Period: Silla Dynasty, 719

This image and NT #82 were made as a pair during the reign of Song-dok (33rd Silla king) in 719. Carved from one piece of stone, the Miruk Posal (Buddha of the Future) was presented to the parents of Kim Chi-song. In 1915 it was brought to Seoul from Kamsan Temple site, near Kyongju. (Dec. 2, 1959)

7. NT #82   Stone Standing Buddha (Amit'abul) from Kamsan-sa Site
                 Location: National Museum, Seoul
                 Period: Silla Dynasty, 719

This stone image of the Amit'abul (Buddha of Western Paradise) was carved from one piece of stone by Kim Chi-song and presented to his family. In 1915 it also was brought to Seoul from Kamsan Temple. (Dec. 2, 1959)

8. NT #83   Gilt Bronze Seated Maitreya (Miruk) Bodhisattva
                 Location: National Museum, Seoul
                 Period: Three Kingdoms, 7th century

This Miruk Bodhisattva has a pose similar to that of NT #78, but is less decorative, not having an elaborate crown and sharply detailed clothing. This Posal of the Future is simpler in style and has a rounder face, faint smile and pierced ears. Except for a simple necklace, its torso is bare. The remnant of a pin on the back of its head shows it used to have a halo. (Dec. 2, 1959)

9. NT #86   Thirteen-storied Marble Pagoda of Kyongch'on-sa
                 Location: Inside of East Gate of Kyongbok Palace, Seoul
                 (see map, p. 20)
                 Period: Koryo Dynasty, 1349

Originally located at Kyongch'on Temple near Kaesong (Koryo Dynasty capital), this pagoda was influenced by Mongolian-style pagodas. It has a three-tiered platform (appearing as three additional stories) with detail in roof rafters and images painstakingly carved in relief. It was ordered constructed to honor a royal wedding during the reign of Ch'ung-mok (29th Koryo king). (Feb. 3, 1960)

10. NT #87   Gold Crown
              Location: National Museum, Seoul
              Period: Early Silla Dynasty, 5th-6th century

There have been many gold crowns discovered in Silla tombs. This one, discovered in 1912, is one of the most elaborate. The Silla tomb was accidentally found during the course of excavation for a house in the heart of Kyongju. This tree-shaped crown with the symbolic deer horns reflects early shaman beliefs. The tomb is called the Gold Crown Tomb because this was the first crown of Silla discovered. (Feb. 3, 1960)

11. NT #88   Gold Girdle with Pendants
              Location: National Museum, Seoul
              Period: Early Silla Dynasty, 5th-6th century

This outstanding example of a Silla girdle came from the same Silla tomb as the Gold Crown (NT #87). It consists of thirty-nine plaques with seventeen pendants suspended from the girdle. At the end of each pendant is a variety of charms of glass, metal, and semiprecious stones. (Feb. 18, 1960)

12. NT #89   Gold Buckle
              Location: National Museum, Seoul
              Period: 5th-6th century

Discovered in 1916 in Pyongyang, it is believed to be of Han Dynasty (Chinese) origin and cannot be considered Korean art. The design includes a large mother dragon with six small dragons. Small pieces of jade are placed into the pattern. (Feb. 18, 1960)

13. NT #90   Gold Earrings
              Location: National Museum, Seoul
              Period: 5th-6th century

This type of earring originated in Han China and came to Silla through Koguryo. Earrings were very popular among Silla nobility, but there is some question as to how they were worn. (Feb. 18, 1960)

14. NT #91   Clay Pottery Vessel in the Form of a Mounted Warrior
              Location: National Museum Seoul
              Period: Early Silla Dynasty, 5th-6th century

A warrior is sitting on a horse, with the tail of the horse serving as the handle of the vessel. The mouth is under the horse's head while a small cup behind the rider is used to pour liquids into the vessel. This pottery piece became the logo symbol of the 5000 Years of Korean Art exibition which traveled through seven cities over a two-year period beginning May 1980. (Feb. 18, 1960)

15. NT #92   Bronze Ewer with Silver Inlay of River, Willow, and Birds
                Location: National Museum, Seoul
                Period: Koryo Dynasty

This ewer or *kundika* is noted for its beautiful silver inlay work of an autumn landscape. Three ducks flying, three ducks on the river and three people under the willow blend in harmony while clouds are depicted on the high neck. Water is poured into this Buddhist ceremonial vessel through the wide-mouthed spout on the shoulder. (Feb. 18, 1960)

16. NT #93   White Porcelain Jar with Underglazed Iron Grap Design
                Location: National Museum, Seoul
                Period: Yi Dynasty, 17th-18th century

During the mid-17th century the use of white procelain was limited. Because of the difficulty in obtaining cobalt blue from the Middle East, the popularity of iron underglaze grew. Some high grade porcelains using iron underglaze were made in the official *punwon* kilns near Seoul though the cobalt blue remained most popular among the royal family. Jars of this period were round and fat with the most popular designs being grapes, grass, hawks, and bamboo. (Feb. 18, 1960)

17. NT #94   Celadon Lobed Vase in the Shape of a Melon
                Location: National Museum, Seoul
                Period: Koryo Dynasty, 12th century

One of the most well known masterpieces of celadon, this vase was discovered in In-jong's tomb (17th Koryo king) in Kyonggi Province. Its body is shaped like a melon with the mouth resembling a melon flower. Vessels of this period are noted for their deep greenish tones. Potters of this period were more concerned with color than with decorative aspects of a vessel. (Feb. 18, 1960)

18. NT #95   Celadon Incense Burner with Openwork Cover
                Location: National Museum, Seoul
                Period: Koryo Dynasty, 12th century

Produced during the same period as NT #94 the design of this censer is extremely elaborate. The lotus-shaped cup rests on the backs of three rabbits. The cover is spherical. Celadons of this early Koryo period were noted for their deep greenish tones. Potters had not yet developed the inlay techniques (Feb. 18, 1960)

19. NT #96   Wine Vessel in the Shape of a Turtle
                Location: National Museum, Seoul
                Period: Koryo Dynasty, 12th century

This celadon piece is probably the finest among the animal-shaped works. The turtle is sitting on a lotus blossom. Wine is poured into a hole on its back and then served through the turtle's mouth. The turtle has a (王) design on its back which is the Chinese character for *wang* (king). It is claimed that this design is found only on male sea turtles. It is amazing to see the refinement of celadon pieces of this period, compared with Buddhist sculpturing, which was rather crude. (Feb. 18, 1960)

20. NT #97   Celadon Vase with Incised Lotus Design
                   Location: National Museum, Seoul
                   Period: Koryo Dynasty, 12th century

The shoulder is big and round whereas the base is narrow and slender. The mouth of the vase is small. The incised design of the lotus blossoms is simple as greater emphasis was placed on color tones. During this earlier Koryo period the inlay techniques, which were first used in Korea, had not yet developed. (Feb. 18, 1960)

21. NT #98   Celadon Pot with Inlaid Peony Design
                   Location: National Museum, Seoul
                   Period: Koryo Dynasty, 12th century

The shape and design of this pot were influenced by Chinese Han Dynasty vessels. The handle on either side is decorated with a lion's face, while between the handles is a large peony design, simple yet bold. (Feb. 18, 1960)

22. NT #99   Twin Three-storied Pagodas from Kalhang-sa
                   Location: Kyongbok Palace, Seoul (see map, p. 20)
                   Period: Silla Dynasty, 758

These two pagodas were moved from Kalhang-sa in North Kyongsang Province to Kyongbok Palace in 1916 and are considered masterpieces of the United Silla period. They were erected by a sister and three brothers, one of whom was Priest On-jok who lived during the reign of Kyong-dok (35th Silla king) in 758. A *yidu* inscription is seen on the upper section of the base of the East Pagoda on the north side of the lane to Kyonghoe-ru. When this pagoda was moved to Kyongbok, a gilt bronze *sari* vase was found. (June 2, 1960)

23. NT #100   Seven-storied Pagoda from Kaesong
                   Location: Kyongbok Palace, Seoul (see map, p. 20)
                   Period: Koryo Dynasty

Moved from Namgae-won near Kaesong in 1915, this pagoda demonstrates a mastery of technique in the setting of the heavy top slabs of rock. At the time of the move to Kyongbok Palace, seven scrolls of Buddhist sutra, beautifully imprinted in silver characters upon blue paper, were found. The scrolls are now on display in the National Museum. (June 2, 1960)

24. NT #101   Stone Relic (*sarit'ap*) Stupa for Priest Chi-gwang
                Location: Kyongbok Palace, Seoul (See map, p. 20)
                Period: Koryo Dynasty, 1085

The *sarit'ap* stupa for Priest Chi-gwang was originally constructed in 1085 at Pobch'on-sa. This pagoda-like stupa is unique in that its lower parts are square shaped. It is richly decorated in carved bas-relief, and appears to have been influenced by Persian art. On the second level there is a carved door with lock, within which the *sari* of Chi-gwang was to have been enshrined. After 1910 this stupa was transported to Osaka, Japan but was later returned to this site. The characteristic features of this monument are the exquisite designs so delicately and superbly carved around the entire body. A tablet constructed for this stupa still stands in Kangwon Province. (June 2, 1960)

25. NT #102   Stone Relic (*sarit'ap*) Stupa for Priest Hong-bop
                Location: Kyongbok Palace, Seoul (See map, p. 20)
                Period: Koryo Period, 1017

Priest Hong-bop studied in China and after returning home became the trusted priest of Song-jong (6th Koryo king). Upon his death the king erected this stupa, naming it Shilsang, at Chongt'o-sa in North Chungchong Province. In 1915 the Shilsang *sarit'ap* was moved from this temple site to Kyongbok Palace. The stupa is exquisitely carved with an octagonal base lotus design, and a spherical central stone with engraved ropes. The central sphere gives the appearance of a ceramic urn. A turtle tablet (Treasure #359) was erected with the stupa and was also moved in 1915. (June 2, 1960)

26. NT #103   Stone Twin Lion Lantern
                Location: National Museum, Seoul
                Period: Silla Dynasty

Of the two lion stone lanterns designated as national treasures, one is located at Pobchu-sa (NT #5) and this one is located in the National Museum. It was first moved to the Toksu Palace in 1931 from Chunghung Mountain Fortress in South Cholla Province; in 1959 it was moved to the Blue House, but a year later was returned to the Toksu Palace where it was located in front of Sokjo-jon. When the new National Museum was completed in Kyongbok Palace it was moved to its present location. Two lions squat on a stone base supporting the lantern with their mouths and front paws. (June 2, 1960)

27. NT #104   Stone Relic (*sarit'ap*) Stupa for Priest Yom-go
                Location: Kyongbok Palace, Seoul (see map, p. 20)
                Period: Silla Dynasty, 844

This stupa is a *sarit'ap* for Priest Yom-go and is claimed to be from Ungbop-sa in Kangwon Province. Believed to contain the *sari* (calcified jewels) of Priest Yom-go of Silla who died in 844, this stupa was moved to Kyongbok Palace at which time an inscription was found inside. Sitting on an octagonal stone base carved with eight lions in relief is a lantern-shaped structure with a tile-like roof. A lotus pattern and *sach'onwang* (four heavenly kings) are depicted on the sides. The carved tile roof is completely realistic. The door design which indicates that this stupa is a *sarit'ap* can be seen on alternate panels. (June 2 1960)

28. NT #105   Three-storied Pagoda from Pomhak-ni, Sanchong-gun,
                 Kyongsang Province
                 Location: Kyongbok Palace, Seoul (see map, p. 20)
                 Period: Silla Dynasty

This typical Silla pagoda was tranferred to Kyongbok Palace from a Buddhist temple at Pomhak-ni in South Kyongsang Province in 1941. Eight panels of carved heavenly generals are depicted on the base stones while four postures of Bodhisattvas are carved on the first story. The entire work with overlapping roof edges is standard form for this period. (June 2, 1960)

29. NT #106   Stone triad of Amit'abul with Inscribed Date
                 Location: National Museum, Seoul
                 Period: Silla Dynasty, 673

Discovered in South Chungchong Province at Piam-sa in September 1960, these images were carved in 673 during the reign of Mun-mu (30th Silla king), who unified Silla (according to inscriptions). The images are carved on a rectangular stone. On the front side are two round columns forming a niche in which the Amit'abul and the two attendants are contained. The faces of the images have been damaged. (Oct. 19, 1960)

30. NT #110   Portrait of Ik-jae
                 Location: National Museum, Seoul
                 Period: Koryo Dynasty, 1319

Ikjae was a great scholar of the late Koryo period. He traveled to China with King Chung-sun and was painted in 1319 by an unknown Chinese artist. (Dec. 20, 1962)

31. NT #113   Celadon Cylindrical Bottle with Willow Design in
                 Underglazed Iron
                 Location: National Museum, Seoul
                 Period: Koryo Dynasty, 13th century

In the third period of Koryo celadon, craftsmanship deteriorated and inlaid designs became rough. Vessels painted in underglaze iron were popular. In most cases designs were crudely simplified, reflecting apathy of the Koryo people during the Mongolian invasion. This cylindrical bottle with a willow tree design is a superb piece giving a more poetic effect than most celadons of this period. This bottle was used for wine. (Dec. 20, 1962)

32. NT #114   Celadon Vase with Inlaid Design of Peonies and Chrysanthemums
Location: National Museum, Seoul
Period: Koryo Dynasty, 12th century

Very similar to National Treasure #94, this vase is also in the shape of a melon. Its body has inlaid designs of peonies and chrysanthemums. For Asia the inlay techniques first developed in Korea. (Dec. 20, 1962)

33. NT #115   Celadon Bowl with Inlaid Floral Design
Location: National Museum, Seoul
Period: Koryo Dynasty, 12th century

This bowl was excavated in Kyonggi Province from the family grave of Mun, who died around 1159. This bowl with inlaid design is the earliest datable celadon piece of this period which developed during the first half of the 12th century. The outside and inside design varies. The addition of inlaid design to Koryo celadon produced a picturesque effect against the color; however, later interest in the inlay techniques caused a gradual neglect and consequent decline of the quality of the glaze color during late Koryo. (Dec. 20, 1962)

34. NT #116   Celadon Ritual Gourd-shaped Ewer and Stopper with Peony Inlaid Design
Location: National Museum, Seoul
Period: Koryo Dynasty, 12th century

This shape was popular during the Koryo period. The color is a fine shade of jade green. The top has flying cranes against a blue sky while the body carries a peony design. (Dec. 20, 1962)

35. NT #119   Gilt Bronze Standing Buddha with Inscription Dating to *yonka* 7th Year
Location: National Museum, Seoul
Period: Koguryo Dynasty, 6th century

This statue was cast in one piece and, except for the tip of the *mandorla,* the image is well preserved due to the condition of the soil it was buried in until its discovery in 1963. The face is slender with a trace of a smile. An inscription on the back reads that the image was cast in the 7th year of *yonka* at a temple in Nakrang (probably Pyongyang area). One thousand images were made with the help of forty priests. This statue was found by a village woman four hundred miles south of Pyongyang at Uiryong-gun, South Kyongsang Province. (Mar. 30, 1964)

36. NT #123   Relic Remains Found in Five-storied Pagoda at Iksan
                Location: National Museum, Seoul
                Period: Late Silla or Early Koryo Dynasty, 10th century

The container found in the five-storied pagoda at Iksan held nineteen gold sheets of the Diamond Sutra with two golden cords, one glass *sari* bottle with gold stopper, two gold saucers, two gold cases with lids, a bronze Buddha, and a small bronze bell with beads. The Diamond Sutra discovered in 1965 was a spectacular find. The gold embossing appears to have been done by use of wooden blocks. (July 26, 1966)

37. NT #124   Stone Seated Bodhisattva From Hansong-sa
                Location: National Museum, Seoul
                Period: Koryo Dynasty, 10th century

Images of the early Koryo period are massive and well-proportioned. This Buddha attendant, made of marble rather than granite, was found at the site of Hansong-sa and is a good example of this period. One of the two existing figures was taken to Japan fifty years ago but was returned to Korea in 1966. The figure has a full feminine body and oval plump face typical of early Koryo (possible Kwanseum Posal, Goddess of Mercy). Later, characterization was marked by large heads and frail bodies. (June 21, 1967)

38. NT #125   Burial Urn with Stone Outer Case
                Location: National Museum, Seoul
                Period: Late Silla Dynasty, 9th century

It was discovered by a Japanese citizen in Kyongju and is considered a masterpiece. This mortuary vessel glazed with green was returned from Japan in 1966. During the Unified Silla period Buddhists and ranking nobles practiced cremation. This type of container was used for the ashes and bones. It has a design of dotted lines with stripes. A granite vessel was also found with the clay vessel and it was the granite vessel that contained this urn. (June 21, 1967)

39. NT #127   Gilt Gold Standing Kwanseum Bodhisattva Holding Bottle
                Location: National Museum, Seoul
                Period: Three Kingdoms, 7th century

This small 8.8 inch statue of Kwanseum (Goddess of Mercy) was discovered in January 1967 east of Seoul (Songbuk-ku, Samyang-dong). Construction workers, while preparing a building site, found this small image. The design indicates that it is probably of Silla origin. The neck does not have the usual three lines under the chin. The image is holding a small bottle and standing on an inverted lotus blossom. With traces of gilt still visible, the image is nearly perfect, with only a small break in the robe just above the feet. (Dec. 19, 1968)

40. NT #131   Original Lineage Record of Yi T'ae-jo
               Location: Cultural Properties Management Bureau, Ch'ang-
               gyong-won, Seoul
               Period: Early Yi Dynasty

This scroll (*Hoch'okwonbon*) now stored in the library of Ch'anggyong-won is the original record showing the ancestral lineage of Yi T'ae-jo (founding king of the Yi Dynasty) from Yi Han who lived during Silla. Yi Han's tomb and ancestral shrine can be seen in Chonju City. The scroll is 22 inches wide and 151 inches long. This record was designated as a national treasure on Nov. 7, 1969.

41. NT #143   Bronze Relics from Taegok-ni, Hwasun
               Location: National Museum, Seoul
               Period: 2-3 century B.C.

These 11 items were discovered in 1971 in Cholla Namdo and consist of the following: Three bronze daggers (longest 33.2cm. in length), Two circular bronze wheel-shaped shaman bells with eight bell-ringing attachments on circumference (12.4cm. in dia.); Two double-ended shaman bronze bar bells; one bronze knife; one bronze axe head (7.7cm. long); and two bronze mirrors (18cm. and 14.5cm. in dia.) (Mar. 2, 1972)

42. NT #166   White Porcelain Vase with Plum and Bamboo Design
               Painted in Underglazed Iron
               Location: National Museum, Seoul
               Period: Yi Dynasty, 16th century

This vase is 40cm. high with mouth 19cm. in diameter. Due to the lack of cobalt blue mineral, Korean potters often resorted to iron and copper for their designs on porcelains. (July 9, 1974)

43. NT #167   Celadon Pitcher in the Shape of a Human Figure
               Location: National Museum, Seoul
               Period: Koryo Dynasty, 12th century

The figure appears to be a religious image, possibly Kwanseum, holding a lotus bud in its hands. The bud serves as the spout and the handle is attached to the image's back. It was probably used in Buddhist ritual. It is 28.2cm. high and 11cm. in base diameter. (July 9, 1974)

44. NT #168   White Porcelain Bottle with Underglazed Copper Design
               Location: National Museum, Seoul
               Period: Yi Dynasty, 15th century

There is some suspicion that this bottle is actually Chinese in origin rather than Korean. Six parallel rings circle the body. Around the center of the body is a plum and chrysanthemum design while on the upper portion is a banana-shaped leaf design pointing upward. The bottle is 21.4cm. high and diameter of base is 7.2cm. (July 9, 1974)

45. NT #182   Gilt Bronze Standing Buddha
                     Location: National Museum, Seoul
                     Period: Late Silla Dynasty

The height of this image is 40.3cm and it has no pedestal. The robe covers both shoulders which is typical of the unification period of Silla. The mudra is palms out with hands raised and lowered. The image was found near Sonsan, Kyongsang Pukdo. (Apr. 23, 1976)

46. NT #183   Gilt Bronze Standing Goddess of Mercy Bodhisattva
                     Location: National Museum, Seoul
                     Period: Three Kingdoms Period

This Kwanseum Posal or Goddess of Mercy was purchased in 1976 and is 32cm. high. It is dated to a period prior to the 7th century. (Apr. 23, 1976)

47. NT #184   Gilt Bronze Standing Goddess of Mercy Bodhisattva
                     Location: National Museum, Seoul
                     Period: Three Kingdoms Period

Along with NT #183 this Kwanseum Posal or Goddess of Mercy was purchased in 1976. It is 34cm. high and dates to about the same period prior to Silla unification. (Apr. 23, 1976)

48. NT #185   Lotus Sutra (Scriptures) Written in Gold
                     Location: National Museum, Seoul
                     Period: Koryo Dynasty

This Sutra was purchased in 1971 in Japan and returned to Korea. It dates to the Koryo Period (10-14th century). The paper Sutra has gold writing and can be folded. Its full length is 31.3 cm. by 11.7cm. (Apr. 23, 1976)

49. NT #186   Gilt Bronze Standing Buddha Image
                     Location: National Museum, Seoul
                     Period: Three Kingdoms Period

The identification of this Buddha image is unclear. Both the hands and feet are missing. It was purchased in 1976 and is 30.3cm. high. (Dec. 14, 1976)

The total National Treasures as of April 1982 are 205 for the entire nation.

Listed Cultural Treasures
(Pomul: Second Rank)
Located in the Palaces

(Note: Designation dates are given in parentheses)

1. T #166   Five-storied Pagoda from Sahyon-sa Site in Hongjae-dong, Seoul
Location: Kyongbok Palace, moved from west Seoul in 1969 (see map, p.20)   (May 3, 1938)
Period: Koryo Dynasty, 1045

2. T #190   Memorial Stone Stupa for Priest Won-gong from Kodun-sa Site
Location: Kyongbok Palace, Seoul (see map, p.20) (Oct.18, 1939)
Period: Early Koryo, 1018

3. T #195   Gilt Bronze Standing Kwanseum Bodhisattva (Goddess of Mercy)
Location: National Museum, Seoul (discovered in 1907) (Dec. 18, 1939)
Period: Paekche Dynasty, 6th-7th century

4. T #196   Gilt Bronze Standing Buddha (Sokkamoni)
Location: National Museum, Seoul (discovered in 1916) (Dec. 18, 1939)
Period: Paekche Dynasty, 6th-7th century

5. T #240   White Porcelain Vase with Openwork Peony Design
Location: National Museum, Seoul (July 31, 1940)
Period: Yi Dynasty, 17th − 18th century

6. T #259   Gilt Bronze Nine-storied Pagoda and two other articles found at Sujong-sa
Location: National Museum, Seoul (June 15, 1942)
Period: Late Koryo, 14th century

7. T #282   Stone Twin Lion Lantern from Kodal-sa Site
Location: Once located at Kodal-sa site in Kyonggi Province, it was brought to Kyongbok Palace in 1959 (see map, p. 20)   (Jan. 11, 1958)
Period: Koryo Dynasty

8. T #325   Nine Treasure Items from Five-storied Pagoda at Songnim-sa, Taegu
Location: National Museum, Seoul (May 21, 1959)
Period: Silla Dynasty

9. T #328   Gilt Bronze Standing Yaksa Yorae (Buddha of Medicine)
Location: National Museum, Seoul (Dec. 2, 1959)
Period: Silla Dynasty, 8th century

10. T #329   Stone Seated Buddha from Kunsu-ni, Puyo
Location: National Museum, Seoul (Dec. 2, 1959)
Period: Paekche Dynasty

11. T #330   Gilt Bronze Standing Maitreya (Miruk) Bodhisattva (Future
Buddha) from Kunsu-ri, Puyo
Location: National Museum, Seoul (Dec. 2, 1959)
Period: Paekche Dynasty

12. T #331   Gilt Bronze Seated Maitreya (Miruk) Bodhisattva (Future
Buddha) with square pedestal
Location: National Museum, Seoul (Dec. 2, 1959)
Period: Three Kingdoms

13. T #333   Gilt Bronze Standing Bodhisattva
Location: National Museum, Seoul, (Dec. 2, 1959)
Period: Three Kingdoms

14. T #338   Gold Crown from Gold Bell Tomb
Location: National Museum, Seoul (Discovered in 1924)
(Feb. 18, 1960)
Period: Silla Dynasty

15. T #339   Gold Crown from Lucky Phoenix Tomb
Location: National Museum, Seoul (Discovered in 1926)
(Feb. 18, 1960)
Period: Silla Dynasty

16. T #340   Celadon *maebyong* Vase with Ginseng Leaf Design in White
and Underglazed Iron
Location: National Museum, Seoul (Feb. 18, 1960)
Period: Koryo Dynasty

17. T #342   Celadon *maebyong* Vessel with Inlaid Plum Design
Location: National Museum, Seoul (Feb. 18, 1960)
Period: Koryo Dynasty

18. T #343   Munyang-jon (Temple Brick Design and Six Other Tile
Patterns)
Location: National Museum, Seoul (Feb. 18, 1960)
Period: Paekche Dynasty

19. T #344   Celadon Kundika Vessel with Reed and Duck Pattern
Location: National Museum, Seoul (Feb. 18, 1960)
Period: Koryo Dynasty

20. T #345   White Porcelain *maebyong*-Vase with Inlaid Peony Design
Location: National Museum, Seoul (Feb. 18, 1960)
Period: Yi Dynasty

21. T #346   Celadon *maebyong*-Vessel with Inlaid Peony Design in
Copper Oxide
Location: National Museum, Seoul (Feb. 18, 1960)
Period: Koryo Dynasty

22. T #347   Celadon *maebyong*-Vessel with Inlaid Fish Design
Location: National Museum, Seoul (Feb. 18, 1960)
Period: Koryo Dynasty

23. T #357   Five-storied Pagoda from Chongdo-sa (*sarit'ap*)
Location: Kyongbok Palace, Seoul, moved here in 1924
(see map, p. 20) (June 2, 1960)50)
Period: Koryo Dynasty, 1031

24. T #358   Twin Three-storied Pagodas from Yongjon-sa (*sarit'ap*)
Location: Kyongbok Palace, moved from near Wonju, 1915
(see map, p. 20) (June 2 1960)
Period: Koryo Dynasty, 1388

25. T #359   Memorial Tablet for Priest Hung-bop from Changt'o-sa
Location: Kyongbok Palace moved in 1915 (see map,
p. 20) (June 2, 1960)
Period: Koryo Dynasty, 1017

26. T #360   Memorial Tablet for Priest Won-rang from Wolgwangsa
Location: Kyonbok Palace, moved here in 1922 (see map,
p. 20) (June 2, 1960)
Period: Silla Dynasty 883

27. T #361   Memorial Tablet for Priest Tae-gyong from Pori-sa Site
Location: Kyongbok Palace, moved here from temple site
in Yangpyong-gun, Kyonggi Province (see map, p. 20)
(June 2, 1960)

28. T #362   Stone Stupa (*pudo*) for Priest Chin-gyong from Pongnim-sa
Location: Kyongbok Palace, moved here in 1919 (see map,
p. 20) (June 2, 1960)
Period: Late Silla Dynasty, 924

29. T #363   Memorial Tablet for Priest Chin-gyong from Pongnim-sa
Location: Kyongbok Palace, moved here in 1919 (see map,
p. 20) (June 2, 1960)
Period: Late Silla Dynasty, 924

30. T #364 Stone Lantern from West Gate of Naju City, Cholla Namdo
Location: Kyongbok Palace (see map, p. 20) (June 2, 1960)
Period: Koryo Dynasty, 1093

31. T #365 Stone Stupa (*sarit'ap*) for Priest Chin-gong and Stone Coffin from Hungbop-sa
Location: Kyongbok Palace, moved here in 1931 (see map, p. 20) (June 2, 1960)
Period: Early Koryo Dynasty, 940

32. T #366 Remains (*sari* and relics of priest) from Three-storied Pagoda at Kamun-sa
Location: National Museum, Seoul (July 1, 1960)
Period: Silla Dynasty, 7th century

33. T #367 Stone Buddha (Amit'abul) with Attendants and Inscription
Location: National Museum, Seoul (Oct. 19, 1960)
Period: Silla Dynasty, 689

34. T #368 Stone Maitreya (Miruk) Bodhisattva (Future Buddha)
Location: National Museum, Seoul (Oct. 19, 1960)
Period: Silla Dynasty, 673

35. T #383 Tonhwa Gate of Ch'angdok Palace
Location: Main Gate to Ch'angdok Palace and Secret Garden (see p. 60-61) (Feb. 5, 1961)
Period: Early Yi Dynasty

36. T #384 Honghwa Gate of Ch'anggyong-Palace
Location: Main Gate of Ch'anggyong-won (zoo), Seoul (see p. 114-115) (June 2, 1961)
Period: Yi Dynasty

37. T #385 Myongjong-jon, Corridors, and Gate in Ch'anggyong-Palace
Location: Main Audience Hall and Entrance of the former Ch'anggyong Palace in Ch'anggyong-won (zoo), Seoul (see p. 114-115) (June 2, 1961)
Period: Yi Dynasty, 1483

38. T #386 Okch'on Bridge of Ch'anggyong Palace
Location: Entrance Bridge after entering Honghwa Gate of the former Ch'anggyong Palace in Ch'anggyong-won (zoo), Seoul (see p. 114-115) (June 2, 1961)
Period: Yi Dynasty, 1483

39. T #452 Celadon Turtle-shaped Water Dropper
Location: National Museum, Seoul (June 21, 1967)
Period: Koryo Dynasty

40. T #453　　　Celadon Wine Cup
　　　　　　　　Location: National Museum, Seoul (June 21, 1967)
　　　　　　　　Period: Koryo Dynasty

41. T #454　　　Gold Bracelet
　　　　　　　　Location: National Museum, Seoul (June 21, 1967)
　　　　　　　　Period: Silla Dynasty

42. T #455　　　Gold Earrings
　　　　　　　　Location: National Museum, Seoul (June 21, 1967)
　　　　　　　　Period: Silla Dynasty

43. T #456　　　Gold Necklace
　　　　　　　　Location: National Museum, Seoul (June 21, 1967)
　　　　　　　　Period: Silla Dynasty

44. T #515　　　Certificate of House Ownership for Princess Sung-jin
　　　　　　　　Location: Bureau of Cultural Properties, Ch'anggyong-won
　　　　　　　　　　　(July 30, 1969)
　　　　　　　　Period: Yi Dynasty

45. T #522　　　Painting of Tosan Sowon (Yi Toe-gye Confucian Study Hall)
　　　　　　　　Location: Bureau of Cultural Properties, Ch'anggyong-won
　　　　　　　　　　　(Aug. 27, 1970)
　　　　　　　　Period: Yi Dynasty

46. T #527　　　Genre Painting Album of Tanwon (Kim Hong-do)
　　　　　　　　Location: National Museum, Seoul (Dec. 30, 1970)
　　　　　　　　Period: Yi Dynasty, 18th century

47. T #568　　　Written Pledge of Seven Lines by Yoon Pong-gil and six
　　　　　　　　　　　personal articles and will
　　　　　　　　Location: National Museum, Seoul (Aug. 16, 1972)
　　　　　　　　Period: 20th century

48. T #588　　　Portrait of Kang Min-soon (government official)
　　　　　　　　Location: National Museum, Seoul (May 16, 1975)
　　　　　　　　Period: Yi Dynasty

49. T #590　　　Portrait of Kang Se-hwang and calligraphy
　　　　　　　　Location: National Museum, Seoul (May 16, 1975)
　　　　　　　　Period: Yi Dynasty

50. T #648　　　Bronze Korean Rifle with "Victory" inscription (67cm)
　　　　　　　　　　　Location: National Museum, Seoul (Dec. 7, 1978)
　　　　　　　　　　　Period: Yi Dynasty (1579)

The total Treasures (*pomul*) as of April 1982 are 730 for the entire nation.

INDEX

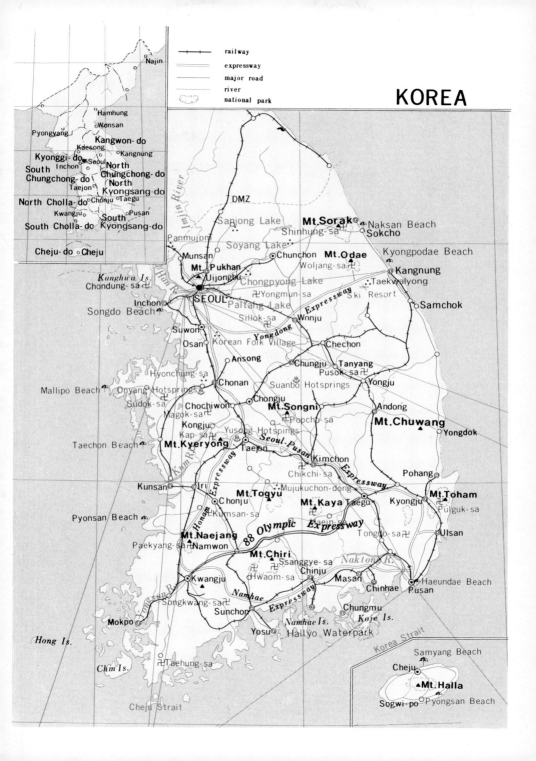

KOREA

railway
expressway
major road
river
national park

Najin

Hamhung
Wonsan

Pyongyang

Kangwon-do

Kyonggi-do
South
Chungchong-do
Kaesong
Inchon
Seoul
Kangnung
North
Chungchong-do
North
Kyongsang-do

Taejon
Chonju
Taegu

North Cholla-do

Kwangju
South
Cholla-do
South
Kyongsang-do
Pusan

Cheju-do ○ Cheju

DMZ

Sanjong Lake
Mt.Sorak
Naksan Beach
Shinhung-sa
Sokcho

Panmunjom
Soyang Lake
Kyongpodae Beach

Munsan
Chunchon
Mt.Odae
Mt.Pukhan
Woljang-sa
Kangnung
Uijongbu
Chongpyong Lake
Taekwalyong
Yongmun-sa
Ski Resort
Inchon
Songdo Beach
Paltang Lake
Wonju
Samchok
Silluk-sa
Suwon
Yongdong
Korean Folk Village
Osan
Chechon
Ansong
Chungju
Tanyang
Pusok-sa
Yongju
Suanbo Hotsprings
Chonan
Hyonchung-sa
Onyang Hotsprings
Chongju
Mt.Songni
Andong
Mt.Chuwang
Mallipo Beach
Sudok-sa
Chochiwon
Popcho-sa
Yongdok
Magok-sa
Kongju
Yusong Hotsprings
Kap-sa
Mt.Kyeryong
Taejon
Kimchon
Pohang
Taechon Beach
Seoul-Pusan
Chikchi-sa
Expressway
Kunsan
Iri
Mt.Togyu
Mujukuchon-dong
Mt.Toham
Honam
Chonju
Mt.Kaya
Taegu
Kyongju
Pulguk-sa
Pyonsan Beach
Expressway
Kumsan-sa
Haein-sa
Tongdo-sa
Ulsan
Mt.Naejang
88 Olympic Expressway
Paekyang-sa
Namwon
Mt.Chiri
Ssanggye-sa
Chinju
Naktong R.
Kwangju
Hwaom-sa
Masan
Haeundae Beach
Songkwang-sa
Namhae
Chinhae
Pusan
Mokpo
Sunchon
Expressway
Chungmu
Hong Is.
Namhae Is.
Koje Is.
Yosu
Hallyo Waterpark

Chin Is.
Taehung-sa

Korea Strait
Samyang Beach
Cheju
Mt.Halla
Sogwi-po
Pyongsan Beach
Cheju Strait

Imjin River
Han R.
Kanghwa Is.
Chondung-sa
Kum R.
Yongsan R.

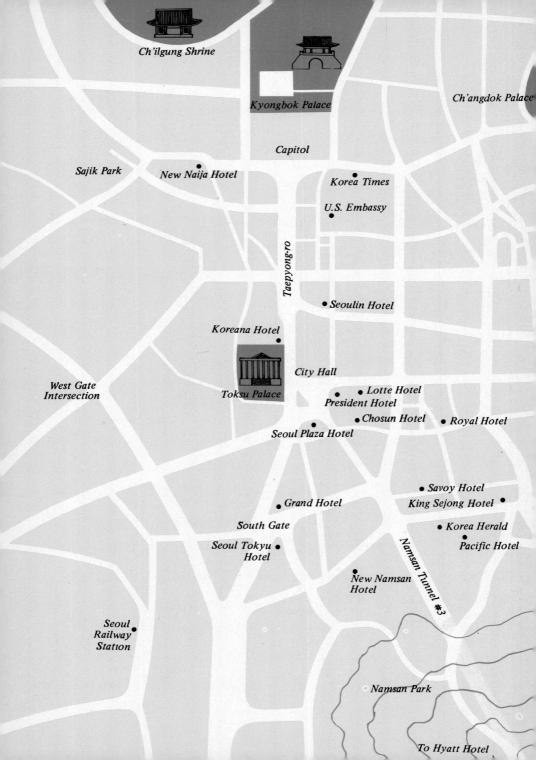

Ch'ilgung Shrine

Kyongbok Palace

Ch'angdok Palace

Capitol

Sajik Park

New Naija Hotel

Korea Times

U.S. Embassy

Taepyong-ro

Seoulin Hotel

Koreana Hotel

City Hall

West Gate
Intersection

Toksu Palace

Lotte Hotel

President Hotel

Chosun Hotel

Royal Hotel

Seoul Plaza Hotel

Savoy Hotel

King Sejong Hotel

Grand Hotel

Korea Herald

South Gate

Pacific Hotel

Seoul Tokyu
Hotel

Namsan Tunnel #3

New Namsan
Hotel

Seoul
Railway
Station

Namsan Park

To Hyatt Hotel

ret Garden

Ch'anggyong-won

Naksonjae

Chongmyo Shrine

DOWNTOWN OF SEOUL

hong-ro

• *Central Hotel*

honggye-ro

Ulchi-ro

East Gate

*National
Medical
Center*
•

Seoul Stadium
•

Toegye-ro
•
oria Hotel • *Korea House*

• *Ambassador Hotel*

Changch'undan Park

• *Hotel Shilla*

Namsan Tunnel #1

Namsan Tunnel #2

About the Author

Edward B. Adams, writer and photographer, was born in Taegu, Korea in 1934 and has been living and traveling in the Orient for over twenty years. His father, George J. Adams, was also born in Taegu and later returned to Korea as a missionary. His grandfather, James Edward Adams who arrived in Pusan in 1895, served as an educator in the Presbyterian Mission.

Mr. Adams spent his childhood years in Andong, the heart of traditional Korea. Returning to Korea as a high school student in 1949, the Korean War tragedy compelled his family to evacuate. In 1965 he came to Korea with the D.O.D. Schools to serve as principal.

Mr. Adams in 1973 with a license from the Korean Ministry of Education founded the Seoul International School and is presently serving as headmaster. With an enrollment of almost 500 students in grades kindergarten through high school, SIS is actively serving as a fully accredited international school in Seoul.

His interest and studies in Korean history and culture have brought him recognition by the Korean government during centennial year of Korean American relations. Over the years he has developed a close relationship with many members of the Yi Dynasty Relatives Association. In *Palaces of Seoul* (revised second edition) Mr. Adams again shares his enthusiasm for the cultural legacy of the Yi Dynasty and the fascination that the palaces of Seoul have held for him over the years.

Other books by author

Through Gates of Seoul Vol. I & II
Korea Guide
Kyongju Guide
Art Treasures of Seoul
Korean Folk Stories for Children
    Two Brothers and Their Magic Gourds
    Woodcutter and Nymph
    Blindman's Daughter
    Herdboy and Weaver
    Korean Cinderella